BLOODY COLONIALS

A SHAMELESS HALLORAN MYSTERY

A NOVEL BY
STAFFORD SANDERS

FROM A STORY BY
STAFFORD SANDERS & TONY LATIMORE

Bloody Colonials
Copyright © 2021 Stafford Sanders
All rights reserved.

ISBN: 978-0-6450394-1-2

Published by A Sense of Place Publishing 2021

No parts of this publication may be reproduced, stored in a retrieval system, or transmitted in any form or by any means, electronic, mechanical, photocopying, recording, or otherwise, without the prior written permission of the copyright owner.

This book is sold subject to the condition that it shall not, by way of trade or otherwise, be lent, resold, hired out, or otherwise circulated without the publisher's prior consent in any form of binding or cover other than that in which it is published and without a similar condition including this condition being imposed on the subsequent purchaser. Under no circumstances may any part of this book be photocopied for resale.

This is the third and final book in the trilogy which began with Terror in Australia: Workers' Paradise Lost and was followed by Hideout in the Apocalypse. They can be read separately or together. They are set against the backdrop of Australia in the early millennial period and largely for legal reasons use novelistic techniques to cover a pivotal point in the nation's history.

Cover design by Jessica Bell
Interior design by Amie McCracken

A catalogue record for this book is available from the National Library of Australia

I dedicate this book to the memory of my parents: Dr John Sanders (1917-2010) – doctor, carpenter, husband, father; lover of the bush, the beach, and a good laugh; and Margaret Sanders (1918-2019) – wordsmith, brilliant mother, and one of the world's true optimists.

WIDE BROWN LAND

Dawn of a new day in strange paradise
We rise with first light as one
We hitch up our chains and we take up our tools
And toil till the long day is done
Far from our homes and the land that we knew
The natural laws we once took to be true
Still the climate's not bad and there's fine lands in view
To work when our sentence has run

We follow their orders, we do what we're told
Don't question the wrong or the right
We're slaves to an empire where sun never sets
'Cause God wouldn't trust them at night
The ground rules keep shifting, the words don't ring true
"Do what we say, never mind what we do"
Still, the water is cool and the sky is bright blue
And we've independence in sight

> *Drowning in sunlight, jumping at shadows*
> *Struggling so hard to understand*
> *This wide brown land*

> *Working on long leads, drifting in dreamworld*
> *Struggling so long to understand*
> *This wide brown land*

You can listen to or download the song, performed by Men With Day Jobs - Track 3 at
http://menwithdayjobs.bandcamp.com/album/dreams-and-tinsel

© 2008 (R.Crundwell/P.Fenton/T.Latimore/S.Sanders)
(Extract from the theme song to the intended feature film of Bloody Colonials)

TABLE OF CONTENTS

PROLOGUE: THE HORSEMAN COMETH 15
1. LAND HO 17
2. EMPIRE BUILDERS 29
3. FIRST CONTACT 34
4. THICKER THAN WATER 42
5. SHAMELESS 50
6. GREAT EXPLORATIONS 58
7. POWER AND POSITION 66
8. SADDLED 73
9. AN UNRESPONSIVE NOTE 79
10. THE BUSINESS OF THE COLONY 83
11. HALLORAN HISTORY 89
12. A GRAND OCCASION 94
13. NOT-SO-GREAT EXPLORATIONS 102
14. THE PLOT SICKENS 111
15. FURTIVE ENDEAVOURS 119
16. TAKEN FOR GRANTED 123
17. DEAD RECKONING 129
18. ALL HELL 133
19. THE FINAL PIECE 143
20. TALLY HO 149
21. THE BOOK OF REVELATIONS 157
22. FULL CIRCLE 166
23. THE HANG OF THE PLACE 170

PROLOGUE: THE HORSEMAN COMETH

A thunder of hooves comes carving at daybreak through the roll and roar of ocean swell crashing against high cliffs.

Wild irregular sandstone crags, they are. Laid down by eons of sedimentary deposit, which ageless motion of wind and wave have scooped and swirled like massive spoonfuls of caramel ice. Far below, huge chunks of this rock, sheared away by the relentless erosion, have crashed to the shelf beneath. There they now lie, like fallen behemoths being slowly consumed in the jagged, frothing jaws of the animal ocean which roars and gnashes and hurls itself repeatedly against the feet of the weatherworn giants.

All this beneath a sky far too blue, a sun far too high and unrelenting than it would appear from the Scottish coast, the White Cliffs of Dover or anywhere else in the Northern Hemisphere. This swirling sea is not the North Sea, the North Atlantic or the Mediterranean. It is, rather, the great South Pacific Ocean.

We have arrived, in the bright dawn of this crisp morning, at the oldest continent in the world: Terra Australis, the Great South Land. Later, of course, called "Australia"; but that will be almost a century beyond this fateful morning in the year 1810.

Listen, the thunder draws nearer.

Around the towering cliffs, a horse bursts into view, ridden at a hearty canter along the narrow rocky clifftop track. It moves with sureness born of familiarity.

Its rider is a man of slight to medium build, perhaps middle-aged, possibly grey-haired, probably clean-shaven, certainly hatless, and wearing a plainish brown riding coat. Though the surroundings are not European, the rider in his manner of dress certainly appears to be from that part of the world.

In the rider's face there is a grim set: brows knitted together just a crease more tightly, jaw set a twitch more firmly, than can be explained solely by the effort of riding. Something is going through the mind of this man. Something that troubles him.

Seeming comfortably set in the saddle and well versed in the twists and turns of the rough track, the horseman digs his heels into the flank and drops his head as his mount approaches a sharpish bend. He shifts his weight automatically in readiness, the horse slowing just slightly to negotiate the oft-taken turn.

But at the very fulcrum of the bend, the rider gives an abrupt and startled cry. A desperate moment of scramble - but purchase is hopelessly lost, centrifugal force doing its inexorable work, body sliding outwards with a rush of fabric and leather.

And whatever concern he had felt up to this point is nothing compared to what he feels now - at finding himself suddenly and finally airborne.

The hapless horseman plummets from view like yet another lump of sandstone towards the rocks far below. Doomed figure followed by something else falling with him, final scream drowned in crash of waves.

Flecked with dreadful crimson, ripples start to spread. And spread.

There now comes the single mournful cry of a seabird – as the horse, having renegotiated its equilibrium following the unexpected loss of burden, comes shuffling to a halt on the clifftop. There it stands, alone in silhouette, whinnying gently towards the unforgiving ocean.

1. LAND HO

In other circumstances, the hearty cry of "Land Ho!" ringing out from the throat of a sturdy young sailor, stripped to the waist atop the crow's nest of a majestic tall ship, might have elicited feelings of excitement, elation or even exhilaration, of a tremendous sense of the achievement of a dream or of the dawning of a life reborn in a bold new world.

In this case, however, all I was able to feel at this exclamation was a rush of numb relief that the interminable blasted journey was finally over and I might soon be back upon dry land at long last.

I hauled my wretched body up from the ship's railing, having just attempted for the latest of God knows how many times to fill the heaving ocean with the contents of my equally heaving stomach. However, having long since lost the entirety of its contents to previous heavings, no more remained within that chamber to be thus emptied.

As I sagged utterly spent against the railing, that hideous and vivid memory once more came flooding back which had so often plagued me upon this long and gruelling voyage. A vision of similar illness gripping me in the midst of previous duties upon other vessels, important duties which did not brook such interruption. Duties as a naval surgeon, so oft embarrassingly cut short by my forced and rushed departures. Operations abandoned midstream to be salvaged by others whose muttered oaths, shaking heads and disapproving looks had followed me angrily as I had fled those rooms to avoid contaminating my colleagues and my poor patient with the erupting contents of my cursed weak vitals.

There now followed an equally ghastly impression of my poor mother, shaking her grey head in dismay - at yet another graphic and irrefutable report of her son's abject failure in the line of naval duty.

This in turn was followed by visions of my most recent nightmare: the long months of rolling, pitching, gut-wrenching discontent, confined for what seemed an eternity in the fetid bowels of a vessel tossed like a scrap of debris upon the mighty and utterly unsympathetic seas. My diet during this voyage, of salt beef, flat bread, biscuits and stale vegetables, ameliorated only by the fact that I had kept so very little of it down. The voyage was not, to be sure, the stuff of which dreams are made.

Shaking these wretched recollections from my pounding head, I now slid gracelessly from the rail and dropped to one knee upon the deck. I winced at the painful crack of emaciated bone against hardened timber. Rubbing the bruised knee, I clambered with some effort to my feet, grasping the rail with both hands, and raised my head to blink blearily through reddened eyes. Out over the side of the ship, its immense cream sails already loosened and fluttering, and away through the mist toward the emerging dark shape beyond.

Yes, no mistaking - it was indeed land. To be precise, the Great South Land. The new jewel in the Crown of the British Empire. Not exactly jewel-like now, it loomed up out of the greyness, a dark, low, craggy and eerily indeterminate presence - but it was land nonetheless. I could not suppress a great rasping sigh at the knowledge that at last my gastric torment would be over.

I had arrived at His Majesty's Colony of Port Fortitude. And, I added to myself with what vehemence I could summon, it was about bloody time.

The problem really started with the Americans. Many problems do seem to start with Americans; but this particular problem was a particular headache for the British Empire in the late eighteenth century - just before this story begins.

The Americans had been part of that great Empire until they turned rather ungratefully against their colonial masters in their impertinent War of Independence – which in 1776 they had the additional temerity to win. They then added insult to insurrection by refusing to allow any more British convicts to be dumped upon what was now, they insisted petulantly, their own sovereign soil.

Damn, thought the British. Now what do we do with all those troublesome convicts? Well, of course we could just hang more of them. That shouldn't be too hard, since hanging was the penalty for a whole array of offences, most of them well short of serious.

The only problem was an infuriating outbreak of humane jury behaviour. Daunted for some reason by the idea of sending cartloads of offenders off to grisly deaths, modern juries were baulking at convicting on capital charges - preferring to find proven only lesser offences carrying sentences of imprisonment.

Damn again. Now what? Well, how about stuffing them all into the overcrowded, rotting hulks of decommissioned ships floating on the River Thames?

In the long term, this clearly would not do. For one thing, the hulks had begun to breed legions of disease-carrying rats – creatures Londoners were just a little edgy about since the Great Plague. Now the rats were breeding at an even faster rate than the Irish Catholics, who had caught the American disease of rebelliousness (or did the Americans catch theirs?). In any case, their similarly ungrateful uprisings were already producing an increasing proportion of the hulks' human inhabitants – though in the face of their heroic posturings, it had to be said, most of these Irish convicts were incarcerated not for politics but for petty crimes: stealing, minor assaults and the like.

In any case, the result was: Double Damn.

It was at this point that some bright spark in His Majesty's Government came up with a seriously original idea: What about sending these prisoners off to the colonies?

Well, yes, of course it had been done before. With the Americans. But this time, it would be different. These prisoners would be sent to the Empire's safely compliant new South Pacific outpost, the Antipodean continent fortuitously discovered in 1770 by Lieutenant James Cook.

Well, to be precise, Cook was not actually the very first to discover the southern continent: that had been done more than a hundred years earlier by the Dutch - who called it "Terra Australis Incognita", the "Great Unknown South Land". So by now it was well past being "Unknown" to the Dutch

– and for that matter, to the French, who had also floated in for a bit of a look; and then there were the Macassan traders popping across fairly frequently from the nearby north; and pirates of course, of various nationalities, who had stopped off for one reason or another before moving on in search of serious looting and pillaging - not seeing much worth looting or pillaging in this particular location.

The British could not, however, contemplate recognising or encouraging in any way the achievements of pirates, even less those of Dutchmen or Frenchmen. No, it was Cook, no mistake, who deserved to be credited with the discovery of the South Land, since he was the first to possess the ceremonial presence of mind to actually plant a national flag and claim the place properly for King and Country.

Well, actually, he was not quite the first to do even this. The French had done the planting and claiming thing – but across on the less hospitable western coast; and anyway, they hadn't followed it up by properly occupying the great island. It remained quite unoccupied when Cook landed in 1770 and quite rightly hoisted the Union Jack.

Well, that is to say, it wasn't occupied by any _civilised_ people. There were natives there of course – but they didn't really count as civilised, since they did no apparent sailing about on the high seas, or planting flags, or anything like that. Thus ran the ingenious legal doctrine of "Terra Nullius" – which asserted that if there were no white Europeans living there, then the place was to all intents and purposes uninhabited – meaning Britain was quite within its rights to march in and take it.

While the colonising officers were under instructions to establish "friendly relations" with the indigines, one cannot remain friendly on an indefinite basis with people who refuse to accept their proper subservient position. After all, as one senior chap in the Colonial Office sagely observed, "If the Almighty had intended the blasted natives to have the place, He would have given _them_ the muskets and _us_ the spears and clubs."

Even worse, He might have given them the lawyers.

So Britain's First Fleet arrived in the South Land in 1788 to begin the arduous business of establishing a penal colony. Soon more ships followed, as the Mother Country began to see the possibilities of expanding her fledgling *outpost beyond mere felonious dumping ground and into potentially prosperous free settlement. Within a decade, British toeholds had begun to spread around the more temperate southern fringes of the continent to virtually all navigable areas of its coastline.*

One notable exception was a particular location, passed over by all explorers to date as being quite unsuitable for human habitation.

From the brief accounts available in the Admiralty records, together with various correspondence sent to my mother and myself prior to my rather forced departure, I had been able to glean a certain amount of information upon the history of Port Fortitude. It was not exactly an encouraging read.

The settlement appeared to have been founded quite by accident - and not, it had to be said, in the most auspicious of circumstances.

The colony had its origins in the early autumn of 1800 - when a British naval vessel, the HMS Fortitude, under Captain George Strickleigh, a Master and Commander of apparently questionable mastery and negligible command, had taken a wrong turning somewhere south of Tahiti and finished hundreds of nautical miles away from its intended destination: the established settlement of Sydney Cove.

Caught in one of the sub-tropical storms abounding in that part of the South Pacific, the Fortitude ricocheted gracelessly off one of the many jagged reefs on this portion of the coastline, and ran aground upon a rocky headland – where it sustained a gaping hole in its hull and was soon battered to pieces by the high seas.

Poor Captain Strickleigh was never seen again. It was believed that he had been asleep below – the written accounts provided no further details of this. In any case the surviving crew, together with a handful of hardy (or possibly foolhardy) settlers, and a smallish gaggle of convicts and their guards, managed to stumble ashore and set up camp with enough provisions to ensure their temporary survival.

Word of this soon reached Sydney Cove by means of reports from passing trading vessels. While perhaps wisely unwilling to negotiate the perilous reefs or hazard a nip into the shallow harbour, they at least passed word to the larger settlement of the evidence they had seen from a distance of some living European presence there – a presence which could only have consisted of the survivors of the Fortitude.

The authorities saw this possibility, if true, as quite fortuitous. The inhospitable nature of the place, remarked upon by explorers and traders - its reefs too hazardous, its bay too exposed and too shallow, its soil too sandy, its insects too profuse, and so forth - had meant that the authorities had been so far unable to persuade anyone to establish any kind of settlement there. Indeed, no settlements existed for some distance either to the north or south. Anything to the west, of course, was assumed to be total wilderness and quite uninhabited – except, perhaps, for natives, who were most likely hostile.

The colonial authorities, then, were eager to grasp this new opportunity of gaining another coastal foothold upon the massive continent – since they lived in constant fear of it being taken away from them by the French. Consequently they had rushed an Acting Governor, a small garrison of troops and a contingent of hardened convicts around the coast from Sydney Cove.

They arrived at the starving survivors' camp in the nick of time, and duly proclaimed it to be from thenceforward His Majesty's Penal Colony of Port Fortitude.

Slowly, like a local sapling snaking raggedly upwards from sandy soil, the settlement had begun to grow.

Unfortunately, by the time I had read these accounts, and forged from their unwelcoming lines even greater misgivings than I had previously held as to what might await me in this forbidding place, it was altogether too late to turn my mother from her singleminded determination to send me there. I pleaded eloquently, apologised profusely for my past failures, promised sincerely to redouble my efforts, and finally questioned with the greatest respect whether it might not be just a tad excessive to compound an offspring's failings and to deny him a chance at redemption by condemning him to the probability of an untimely death – whether from the perils of the voyage, or from a native attack, or perhaps from some dreadful tropical disease. Or indeed all of the above.

Alas, it was to no avail. Mother was unmoved and quite resolute. My place in the family heritage must be salvaged, she determined, and salvaged it would be; and if I should perish in the attempt, then it were better to perish bravely than to live on in lily-livered disgrace.

I had no choice, then, but to grit my teeth and accept my fate. I was to be transported to this God-forsaken spot, for - who knows? - possibly the term of my natural life. Given what I had read of Port Fortitude, most likely a term of no great duration.

Still, at least I had survived the blasted voyage. So far, as they say, so good.

On the craggy headland above the grey mist stands a solitary figure – the first to view the arrival of the ship.

She is Polly Dawes, a convict maidservant in plain sturdy working dress, apron and cotton bonnet. She has been up and about already for some hours, rising before daybreak to pump water from the well, to be used in the washing of clothes and the watering of chickens and pigs.

She's just completed this last chore, and has emerged onto the grassy headland between Government House and the cliffs, full washing basket under one arm, empty scrap tin in one hand, empty water bucket in the other.

Bleedin' pigs, she thinks with annoyance. Third one this month that's got out, an' I don't suppose we'll ever see that one again, run off into the bush like the others. So there's one more dinner that'll have to be filled out with potatoes an' greens an' whatever else we can grow in this rubbish soil. Oh well. Nothin' to be done.

Now she stops as something in the distance catches her eye. She squints towards the horizon and her eyes widen slightly. She takes a step towards the clifftop and puts down the bucket and tin, one grubby sleeve mopping sweat from her ruddy cheek.

Ah, she nods, the ship is in at last. Its tall, pale sails loom unmistakeably up out of the ocean mist as it inches its way slowly around the perilous reef and into the shallow bay.

Polly stands, stares at the ship for a moment, removing her bonnet to swat a stray fly from her cheek. About bleedin' time too, she thinks. Now maybe we might get some little rise in the food rations at last. Maybe they've brought over some more pigs, an' all.

Well… no point standin' around here when there's work to be done, she determines, and no doubt there'll be a good deal more rushin' about at Government House once that lot get ashore, what with all the unloadin' and cartin' about an what-have-you. All those men with their grand schemes, lots of shoutin' an' everythin's the most important thing that ever there was, an' it must all be done by about yesterday, or there's hell to pay. An' if it's not done, well, most likely it'll be some poor convict that gets the blame. She shakes her head slowly.

She turns, leaving the bucket and scrap tin for the moment where they lie in the shallow heath. She gathers her washing basket in both hands, and turns again towards the clothesline.

But as she does so, behind her she hears a noise. No, more than just a noise, a definite and human sort of noise. Well, barely human – and, she shudders, recognising the sound, most decidedly unwelcome. The sound is a low, rasping clearing of the throat, exaggerated to the point of stagecraft. It is a noise that could only come from one person.

Fixing a politely bland expression onto her healthy features and summoning what civility she can muster, Polly turns to face the Reverend Ezekiel Staines, colonial chaplain.

"Mornin', Reverend", she intones steadily.

The Chaplain smiles, his ineffectively shaven jowls creasing into a leer above the ever-present off-white clerical collar - which looks very much the worse for having had a number of fluids spilled down the front flaps of it, over the significant period since it appears to have seen any hint of soapy water.

"Lovely morning, my dear", opines the Reverend in a kind of rasping sing-song - rather akin, thinks Polly, to the sound of a badly-oiled gate. Then he adds with the leer gaining in intensity: "And, I may say, a lovely vision to grace it." He flutters his eyelashes and almost drools.

My God, she observes with disgust, even his lashes are oily. Over the involuntary turning of her stomach, she forces another barely tolerant half-smile which she works hard to ensure is not accompanied by any visible rolling of the eyes. She satisfies herself with a tone of firm but gentle reproof, trying not to make it sound the least bit playful, coquettish or otherwise encouraging, but merely to truncate further conversation as deftly and politely as possible.

"Now now, Reverend," she says, in the tone of a kindly but firm governess, "that'll do."

And as she turns away from him towards the washing line she adds under her breath, unheard by him: "Pig."

For a moment the chaplain considers following her; but something in the quiet steel of her rebuff deters him. He narrows his eyes and smiles ruefully, thinking to himself: *Bit of a wild one, that one. All that scuttlebutt about the fate that reportedly befell the last man who tried to force his attentions upon her. Had to be shipped home in two separate vessels, according to Halloran the stablehand.* Mind you, the Reverend sneers to himself, *anything coming from that highly dubious source would need to be taken with a most generous pinch of salt.*

Staines shakes his head and watches with ill-disguised prurience Polly's generous hips swinging backwards and forwards as she pegs the washing out upon the line.

Yes, he thinks, *after five years in the colony it is high time I found myself a nice little wife.* And then on reflection: *But possibly one in need of a little less taming than she. High-spirited, that is the word for her. And while there can be certain… advantages in that, I am not at all sure that she would respond to the requisite degree of discipline from a strong husband and moral guardian such as myself — no matter whether or not the Holy Bible might instruct her that man must rule and woman must obey.*

Still, one must not be choosy, he warns himself, *what with men outnumbering women in the colony by a proportion of no less than seven or eight to one. Ah,* he thinks with a sigh, *the many trials cast by the Almighty in the path of us mere mortals.*

He ruminates upon this for a moment, takes a deep breath, turns and shuffles away, inspired by his spiritual ponderings to begin a rather tuneless mumbling of one of John Newton's popular hymns of the time, "The Prodigal Son":

> *Afflictions, though they seem severe,*
> *In mercy oft are sent…*

Newton, of course, had been associated with the campaign against slavery — but Staines does not hold this against him. After all, to a good Christian it *does seem wrong to haul some poor African half way around the world in the bowels of a ship and turn him into a beast of burden.*

No, far better to use the Irish for that. At least they understand what you are yelling at them. Well, almost.

As the Reverend warbles on, his eyes have drifted to the Heavens and away out to sea. All at once he stops, squints into the morning haze. Distant cream shapes flutter majestically into the bay.

Ah, he thinks, the ship has come in at last. His mood brightens immediately at the prospect of the new parishioners this vessel may bring — hopefully a good proportion of them female.

With a great deal more spring in his step now, the Chaplain turns and totters happily off past Government House towards the main street.

Through heavy eyelids half-closed against the bright glare, someone else now observes the ship as it drops anchor out in the bay and the longboats are prepared for the bridging of the remaining distance to the shore.

This observer has only moments ago emerged from the track leading down from the settlement, and now props his ample frame against a navigation post at the top of the dunes overlooking the beach. He puffs with the exertion of this activity as he wipes the sweat from his brow and peers from under a ragged straw hat towards the ship, which sits placidly at anchor in the early morning calm of the bay.

Well now, he thinks, sure an' that'd be a welcome sight. An' not before time, too.

He's reminded of a similar day — must be about just about seven years past now — when he himself arrived on a similar vessel, and from the same port of origin: Portsmouth. He recalls the surge of mixed emotions with which he had at first set foot upon these golden sands. Such a long way, so far from everything he was familiar with. And into a life of such hard labour in such strange surroundings.

Well, he thinks, not all that hard, really, not the way I've managed to arrange most of it. At the end o' the day I'm still standin', he thinks - unlike some. I've not fared all that badly from it, all things considered - not compared with what might'a been. Doesn't stack up all that bad, really, he concludes, against the hard realities o' life on the back streets o' Dublin. Wouldn't be tradin' my lot for those back there. Not now.

Still, he thinks, can't be countin' me chickens at this point. Not out o' the woods yet. Still need to be playin' me cards carefully. 'Specially with what I know about...

His gaze has drifted slowly across the horizon and has run up hard against the dark foot of South Head cliff, its craggy profile standing imposing against the brittle glare.

For one startling moment, there's a terrible flash in his mind's eye of a dark shape (or is it two, a larger and a smaller one?) hurtling with a scream towards oblivion. He blinks, rubs his eyes, shudders. The vision is gone.

Now listen, lad, he reprimands himself, don't you go back there. You get that business well and truly out of yer mind, if you know what's good for yer. Nothin' to be gained by mullin' over that. Nothin' at all.

He narrows his eyes and directs them purposefully back across the dazzling bay towards the ship. He peers with interest at the longboats. One has set off towards the rough jetty at the southern fringe of the bay just below his position. Wonder who's comin' ashore off this one, he thinks. And with an inadvertent licking of the lips: an' what quality o' merchandise might be aboard.

He rubs his hands together and starts to whistle a rather comical little tune. Were it more recognisably whistled, it might be identified as an Irish jig.

After what seemed an interminable negotiation of the difficult harbour entrance, the ship had creaked its way slowly and mercifully to a dead halt. It now stood finally at anchor in the large bay.

Several longboats had been lowered alongside and an assortment of ropes and ladders dropped to meet them. I had not dared to watch as with the most remarkable dexterity, the sailors had set to work, conveying luggage and passengers into the boats. I had hung back while most of these had set off for the jetty. I now inched gingerly towards the railing and forced a quick glance downward towards the last of these rather unstable-looking vessels, now bobbing like a cork in the briny in the shade of the ship's flank, far below where I stood apprehensively awaiting instructions.

I noted with some relief that my own trunk – filled with my clothes, books, medical equipment and assorted other odds and ends - was among the items stacked at the stern of the longboat. Various passengers, having scrambled gleefully down the rope ladder, were now seated therein: a small, motley cluster of settlers of diverse ages, all staring upwards toward the rail of the ship, behind which I remained perched in a state of some reluctance like a long-confined prisoner, pale and skeletal, blinking through the bars towards an uncertain freedom.

"Come on, Doctor, down you come, sir", shouted a hefty sailor in what he evidently hoped was a confidence-inspiring tone of jovial encouragement; but his voice came from so far below that it gave the impression of rising mockingly from the depths like the cry of some ghostly denizen of Davey Jones' locker – or indeed Mister Jones himself, inviting the unwary sailor to descend into his watery clutches.

"Down you come"? Easier said than done, I thought. Rope ladders had never been my stock in trade - let alone those dangling from the sides of sea vessels, lurching in sub-tropical swells, into even more wildly lurching and perilously over-laden longboats.

Nevertheless it appeared the thing would have to be done, and better sooner than later. Yes, I determined, best get it over with. Now is the moment, I thought. Yes indeed, I decided, let us without further…

"Come on now, sir! Before the next change of tide, if ye please!" Hoots of laughter from the other sailors and passengers at this.

I gritted my teeth and took firm hold of the ladder with both hands, heaved myself awkwardly over the side and, not daring a seaward glance, started to inch painstakingly downwards, scraping and bumping my already bruised knee against the side of the ship. And bruising the other one to match it, along with both elbows for good measure. In this fashion I made my way towards my destination, bobbing unsteadily such a daunting distance below.

After what seemed hours of diligent scrambling, I had very nearly attained the relative safety of the smaller vessel - when, perhaps a little over-eager to reach it and the promise of dry land beyond, I slipped from the ladder and fell with a squawk and a splash into the swirling water between ship and boat.

I rose paddling wildly to the surface, choking and spluttering, my only thought at this instant being how terribly farcical it was to have survived such a long and gruelling journey, only to drown within a few oarstrokes of the shore. In the rush of water churning around my head I could almost hear Davey's voice, laughing in mockery: Ha ha, got another one. Down you come, doctor. All the way down.

In the next instant, however, I felt several strong hands grasping my arms and coat, and I was hauled most unceremoniously up over the gunwale and into the longboat. There I lay on my back with my legs kicking helplessly in the air like some half-drowned insect, to the unkind guffaws of sailors and passengers alike.

Slowly I heaved myself onto the end of a box and sat there exhausted and bedraggled, dripping and gasping for breath atop the luggage - as the oars were manned and we set off for the beach. Each new lurch threatened to bring up once more the now merely theoretical contents of my stomach.

2. EMPIRE BUILDERS

Along the dusty street that runs in front of Government House, a rather impressive couple come sauntering grandly, arm in arm.

These two are dressed to the nines. He in broad-brimmed black hat and tie, dark waistcoat, frock coat with silver buttons, and ruffled shirt-front. She, the taller of the two, looms above him in full-length brocaded and billowing bustled gown, buttoned high at the neck, and topped by an enormous floral hat and ornate frilled parasol. Despite the shade offered by this, both are perspiring visibly, their outfits clearly excessive in the baking South Pacific heat.

As these two very fine personages draw level with the rough stone façade of Government House, the Reverend Staines emerges from behind it. He falters in his step as he catches the gaze of the grand couple, and grins awkwardly and perhaps a trifle guiltily. They saunter to a stop in front of him.

"Good day to you, Reverend Staines" comes the cultured and just faintly European-accented voice of the lady. She is a woman of stature and some beauty, mature and somewhat hardening though it appears. A droplet of perspiration clings to the end of her aquiline nose – down which she looks imperiously at the chaplain as he performs his characteristic gesture of fiddling with his besmirched clerical collar, pulling it up nervously in a manner perhaps symbolic of his constantly faltering struggle to carry the personal burden of its moral responsibilities. He twitches slightly and lowers his head in what he fondly imagines to be a charming, chivalrous posture, but which manages only to achieve the visible status of fawning.

"Ah… good morning, Lady Anastasia… er, Colonel McMurdough", he adds quickly, though never taking his batting eyes from the lady. "Lovely day for it."

The lady merely inclines her head in a response of polite and dignified elegance; but the Colonel returns the greeting with haughty blankness upon his rather broad, nondescript face. "For what?"

Anastasia rolls her eyes with exasperation, hissing through clenched teeth to him: "It's a figure of speech, Montague…"

Her husband nods ponderously in something short of full understanding, figures of speech being definitely not his forte.

The Chaplain now sees an opportunity for further oiliness and flutters his eyelashes with renewed vigour at the lady, as he oozes the double-entendred answer: "For delighting in the delicate beauties of Creation, Milady."

She raises one eyebrow ever so slightly and smiles, lowering her eyes with an exaggerated demureness of acknowledgment. In the severely limited social environment of the colony, such flattery must be taken wherever – and, more to the point, from whomever - it may.

Colonel McMurdough meanwhile raises his own eyebrow, rather less subtly; but he's apparently not quite sure whether to be suspicious about the turn of the conversation, or how suspicious to be – such finer judgments of human motivation also not being his forte.

"Indeed", he finally manages to respond with what he imagines to be the subtlest hint of warning – given that he is not quite certain whether any warning, or how much warning, is warranted.

At this point the Reverend, deciding this banter has probably been pursued as far as he dares, abruptly changes his tone to one more businesslike. "Ah well," he blurts, "must be getting on. Got a flogging to attend to."

And rubbing his hands together with barely disguised glee at this prospect, and with no sense of irony at the rather contradictory shift from the delicate beauties of creation to the brutal realities of corporal punishment, he turns to go; but then stops short as he remembers: "Oh, by the way, the ship has come in."

"Has it now?" responds the lady with a sharp narrowing of the eyes; and her husband reacts a good beat later, still only half way towards taking in the information, speed of comprehension being yet another item in the fairly large catalogue of intellectual skills which, we're discovering, are not his forte:

"Ah. Indeed."

To the McMurdoughs, word of the ship's arrival is something of a double-edged sword. It's partly good news, carrying the prospect of addition to their livestock, crops and other items helpful to the furtherance of their prosperity - which is, not unfair to say, the paramount consideration for both of them. And then there are those items of expensive furniture, fine clothes, spirits, gourmet delicacies and other trappings of their station. Some of these have been long awaited – Anastasia in particular feeling their absence keenly, being a woman accustomed to the very best that life has to offer.

But the ship's arrival also carries the possibility of contact from Europe; and they both feel vaguely apprehensive – he rather more vaguely than she – of anything untoward which might have followed them here from the old life, anything they might prefer had been left well behind.

"Good day to you" lubricates the Reverend's departing bulk, and they half-heartedly return the formality, still partly occupied in exchanging the apprehensive look about the ship's arrival.

Staines hurries off past Government House – through the window of which, there are figures in animated conversation.

Sir Henry Blythe, second Governor of His Majesty's Colony of Port Fortitude, sits before a large gilt-framed portrait of himself mounted on the wall behind his enormous oak desk.

The Governor is attempting in vain to work on various documents relating to an array of colonial management business. He is being frustrated in this endeavour by an expensively-dressed and very attractive young woman who is pressing him in a simpering voice while she toys with a scale model of elaborate buildings and bridges mounted on a table in the centre of the amply-proportioned room.

"Oh go on, Papa," she whines, "just a little dinner party. It's so boring here, and it's been positively ages since we had a dinner party."

The Governor barely looks up, continuing to write, brow furrowed with battling concentration. He responds with gruff matter-of-factness: "About six weeks, I believe."

"Yes, well, six weeks in this place is an eternity!" *she bleats.* "Honestly, it's a social desert. And anyway, that dreadful 'Lady' Anastasia" (the 'Lady' is placed by the young woman in the most derisive of audible quotation marks, accompanied by a grimacing parody of a smile) "has had another of <u>hers</u> since then. You don't want us to be shown up by <u>her</u>, do you?"

The Governor shrugs non-committally at this, not unduly concerned by the finer points of such competition. Frustrated by this lack of suitable response, his daughter half-turns and swats petulantly at the model, slightly dislodging a balsa-wood roof. Finally and irreversibly distracted from his work, and concerned for the wellbeing of the architectural plan, the Governor scrambles to his feet and emerges hurriedly from behind the desk to interpose himself between his colonial vision and its impetuous attacker.

In real life, Sir Henry is considerably less physically imposing than his portrait makes him appear. He is in fact, it must be said, rather short.

"Yes, well my dear Felicity," he harrumphs impatiently, "it's a little early to be making socialising quite our top priority…" He replaces the model roof and plants his diminutive frame firmly between his daughter and the imperilled work "… since I am, after all, supposed to be running a penal colony – with or without the proper degree of loyalty from my subordinates, or anything approaching the requisite level of support from the Colonial Office."

Now it's his daughter's turn to brush aside irritating trifles. "Well," she retorts with a pout, "you certainly gave me the impression the social life here was a high priority when you went to such lengths to persuade me to come rushing out here the moment I had completed Finishing School. As I recall, you said…"

But her father is mercifully spared the reiteration of his own arguments at that time by a knock at the door.

"Enter!" barks the Governor. And Polly the maidservant comes in, back from her work outside with the pigs and the washing. She curtseys perfunctorily.

"Ship's come in, Your Excellency", she informs him.

"Ah." His eyes sharpen. This is welcome news indeed to Sir Henry: the ship will bring keenly-awaited settlers, troop reinforcements, livestock, goods – particularly some of the finer building materials not available from the limited natural resources of the colony. Especially not from this particularly limited part of it.

His daughter, too, cheers up immediately at the news. "Oh, at last," *she squeals, clapping her hands together with childish enthusiasm,* "my pianoforte! At least now I can have some decent music."

"Indeed you shall," *agrees her father,* "and not only that, but some new company as well. Your cousin, our new colonial surgeon, will be on board the..."

But Felicity ignores him, her mind on one thing only. She brushes her father lightly aside and turns to her convict maidservant: "Get some men down there straight away to bring it up at once - and mind they take special care with it."

"Yes, milady", *mutters Polly, with long-suffering weariness, turning towards the door.*

The Governor is long inured to the reality of being unable at the best of times to command his daughter's attention for more than a few moments. He makes no further attempt to do so - instead returning to more practical matters. "Oh, and send Major Bascombe in, would you," *he directs Polly's departing form.*

He retreats with some relief behind the safety of his desk as the convict girl scurries out, followed by Felicity, who prattles instructions at her to which she is paying just as much attention as she needs, but no more.

"The ship has come in!" "Ah, the ship is in, thank God!" "It has arrived at long last – the ship!" *Word now spreads like a forest fire throughout the settlement.*

Imagine for a moment the excitement of waiting for a loved one to return from an absence of a day or a week. Or for the arrival in the post of letters from family or friends. Confirmation of new employment. A birthday present. A long-awaited purchase.

Then imagine such anticipation accumulating over several months – and in the absence of any other form of long-range communication. Now we begin to understand the magnitude of impact of the cream sails' arrival in the bay of Port Fortitude. This ship is a thinly-stretched lifeline. It bears the preservation of life and health, the reuniting of families and friends, and the maintenance of contact with what for many is still thought of as "home".

Nevertheless, with whatever enthusiasm the ship may be greeted by some, there is at least one of its passengers who will be more than pleased to see the last of it.

3. FIRST CONTACT

The longboat, having with a small lurch negotiated the task of bumping its bow up against the jetty (and I having negotiated the suppression of further retching at this movement), settled unsteadily into place against the rough timber posts.

I may have been the last to have been cajoled aboard the boat, but I was hell-bent upon being the first to depart from it. One final taste of the damned sea awaited me, however, as I attempted to scramble from the boat onto the rudimentary wharf. Again in my haste to be ashore, my foot caught the gunwale and I was propelled with an exasperated cry, sprawling headlong over the side, cannoning off the mooring post and sliding once again down into the briny.

Fortunately I maintained my grasp upon the post and managed to haul myself (this time without assistance) up onto the rickety structure, where I lay amid fresh howls of mirth, spitting mouthfuls of salt water. I scrambled to my feet and stood dripping upon the timbers as my trunk was dumped alongside me. I mumbled a word of thanks to the sailors as they and the other passengers scampered nimbly past me and off along the jetty, still chortling at my clumsiness. Then I drew a deep breath of humid, salty air, narrowly suppressed one last retch, and turned towards the beach, squinting into the bright sunlight. A few lurching steps along the creaking jetty and onto the golden sand, and there I was – upon dry land at long, long last.

I looked up – and at once a most extraordinary sight confronted me.

A grand piano stood in full glory upon the sand, glistening with salt spray. Fearing that delirium from the gruelling voyage might have addled my brains, I shook my head and blinked – but there it was still, standing grandly on its three carved legs upon this remote Antipodean beach. From somewhere in the back of my mind I fancied I could hear a Scottish waltz playing dimly. That, however, was definitely my imagination, I determined – while the piano itself was assuredly not so, remaining in place even after I had shaken my head with what vigour I could manage without renewing the nausea.

I must have stared at this vision for some moments before a brace of hefty fellows rushed up past me and surrounded the instrument, attaching ropes to it with a flutter of argued cross-instructions to each other. Slowly they hauled upon the cords and, staggering under the piano's weight, bore it slowly off up the beach.

I watched them depart over the dunes into the strange and tangled vegetation. Then I looked about me once more.

Leaning against a painted post some distance away was a solitary, scruffy-looking, rather pot-bellied fellow wearing a dirty and tattered arrowhead-patterned shirt, baggy britches and a large and very ragged straw hat slung low across his brow, obscuring much of his face.

I moved up the dune towards him and hailed him. He looked slowly up, jowled and stubbled face half hidden beneath the hat, and I could not help imagining myself being rather smartly sized up as there came a gravelly but lilting Irish brogue:

"What can I be doin' for you, sir?"

"Ah, could you direct me to... er, Government House, if you please?" I enquired.

He turned and waved one finger lazily up the beach towards the dunes. "That'd be straight over the dune, sir. Just follow the track. Yer can't miss it."

I followed the vaguely indicating digit up the sloping sand and saw behind it a steepish, wooded rise. Then I looked back uncertainly at my heavy trunk, still sitting upon the jetty, and ventured to inquire: "Er... would my trunk be safe here, for the time being?"

The fellow glanced quickly at the trunk. Then he turned to me with a reassuring though still only partially visible smile under the shreds of hat. "As houses, sir," he said. "As houses."

"You'll… see to it?"

"In person, sir," he reassured. "Just you leave it to me."

Something in the tone of his voice encouraged me to follow this course. I nodded in acknowledgment to him, and the ragged hat nodded back, the face remaining mostly hidden. Then he turned slowly back toward the bay and remained propped against the post, looking out to sea, as I drew in my breath and headed past him.

Slowly I trudged to the top of the dune, stumbling upon the heavy sand - as what the sailors had referred to laughingly as my sea-legs sought to adjust to the now unfamiliar lack of any lurching motion beneath.

As I concentrated upon this simple but challenging task, I was startled by a sudden noise nearby and I turned suddenly at the sound of a loud lisping bellow from somewhere above: "Look out there, stand aside!"

I leapt out of the way barely in time to avoid being trampled upon by what I at first thought to be a horse. Certainly it was a hooved creature, sandy brown in colour. I soon realised, however, that it was not the right shape for a horse - being larger and distinctly humped in the back, with an extraordinarily long neck and strange visage featuring large lazy eyes and a set of bulbous pouting lips. This, I knew from a previous voyage to the East, was a camel.

Perched atop this beast was a wild, bearded figure in a very dusty khaki uniform and a pith helmet. He cast a fierce and manic glance down at me, waving me aside with brute imperiousness as he swatted the flies away with a gold-rimmed fan. Behind him, draped over the camel's hump, was an assortment of baggage, with various spears and an array of carved and shaped wooden implements jutting out in all directions.

Sauntering along beside, the creature's bridle in hand, was an ebony-skinned man whom I took to be a native of these parts, bare-chested but wearing rough baggy trousers tied with a rope belt. He turned with a desultory shake to his unkempt shock of curly black hair, and gave me a broad and vague grin, the large white teeth in stark contrast with the shiny black face surrounding them.

This eccentric procession moved past me with a slow rumble of hooves and a rattle of implements. I stared open-mouthed at their disappearing forms heading down behind the next dune.

Then, wondering what bewildering vision could possibly await me next, I looked down the landward side of the dune for the opening between the scrubby trees to the rough-hewn track leading up to the settlement.

The Governor, still in his office, is moving objects around within the miniature world of his model. He rubs his chin, pondering the placement of some future ambitious construction. Casts his eye absently about, allowing it to linger for a moment on his own painted image high on the wall.

My predecessor might not have had the stamina to endure here, he thinks – poor chap lasted a mere two years before succumbing to a weak heart fuelled by an excess of liquor. I, however, am most assuredly made of sterner stuff. I will show them. Subconsciously he draws himself up straighter.

A knock is heard. Sir Henry frowns at this intrusion into one of his increasingly rare quiet moments.

"Enter! Ah, Bascombe."

Major Geoffrey Bascombe, the Governor's Adjutant, enters. He wears the red coat, white breeches and crossed sashes of His Majesty's Army Corps. He carries a sheaf of papers and a set of enormous sideburns. Well, he's not so much carrying the sideburns – they have, in fact, more of the appearance of carrying him.

He takes a few starched steps forward and salutes stiffly, chin thrust prominently forward as if to provide a base for the sideburns. The Governor returns the salute perfunctorily.

"The ship has come in," *Blythe informs him,* "with, I trust, our new surgeon aboard. Make sure his quarters are in readiness at the barracks, would you."

"Sir." *Bascombe thrusts some papers under the Governor's nose. Blythe signs them without appearing to look at them. His tone carries a quiet but firm warning, eyes engaging the direct gaze of the Major.*

"And Bascombe… try and keep him out of trouble, would you?"

A slight grimace crosses the face of the Major as he retrieves the signed papers. Just what I need, he thinks – more work. As if my list of duties was not already sufficiently onerous, without having the Governor's babysitting added to them. "I shall do the best I can, sir", he undertakes with the requisite evasive respectfulness. He salutes again and heads for the door.

"Mmm. Not sure I find that particularly reassuring," mutters the Governor. He runs a hand over his thinning pate and swivels back to the relative security of his model colony.

Glancing back in the direction of the jetty from the top of the sand dune, I could see the unloading of the ship proceeding languidly, if noisily.

A number of people had emerged onto the jetty and appeared to be taking a proprietorial interest in the various items being unloaded.

Most prominent among these observers, I noticed one very grand-looking couple, of whom the lady, a statuesque woman carrying a parasol - appeared to be exuding a most commanding presence. She was issuing instructions to sailors and labourers as to the transfer of livestock and other goods with the imperiousness of an army general.

A great many boxes and barrels marked FLOUR and SUGAR – and many more marked RUM - were being hauled ashore; also visible were cages of pigs and goats, together with pots of plants labelled GORSE, LANTANA, PRICKLY PEAR and something called "BITOO BUSH".

I noticed now what appeared to be a number of large rats which came scurrying out of holes in boxes or bags and darting off into the bush. They were pursued by several domestic cats of various shapes and sizes. These in turn were chased half-heartedly by shouting men making cursory attempts to recapture them among the impossibly dense foliage, before returning with resigned shrugs to their unloading.

I half-slid down the sand and into the gap between the trees marking the base of the rough stony track which wound upwards into the strange coastal forest. Turning to either side I beheld, at close quarters now, the strange forms of the local vegetation.

As sand gave way to rocks and soil, there emerged low clumps of reeds and grasses, among clusters of succulent groundwort, clinging to the rear of the dunes. Further into the forest were scattered an assortment of sprouting palms and ferns, some erupting like bright green volcanoes from stumpy black bulbs. The effect was altogether prehistoric. Exotic birds screeched and squawked overhead. One of these was a ragged greyish one with a large bill. Alighting upon a nearby bough, feathers standing erect upon its head like an American Indian headdress, it gave me a roguish, one-eyed appraisal and proceeded to emit as I passed what I can only describe as the deranged cackle of a fiend from Hell.

As I made my way up the track and further away from the beach, from the greenery on either side of the track rose the trunks of several varieties of tree - some of them quite unlike any that I had ever seen. Smooth of bark but wantonly crooked, apparently shunning a direct climb toward the daunting sunlight which their scrappy foliage failed to shield fully. These ghostly grey-white apparitions instead twisted and turned vaguely upward in a variety of sinister shapes, seeming at times to extend great gnarled claws over my head.

In amongst these were smaller, darker trees in which nestled the most alarming seed-pods, enormous, bulbous blackish things looking for all the world like deformed heads with bulging eyes and bloated lips, seeming to stare and leer at me from between the fronds of shaggy foliage.

Looking up at these hideous heads amongst the spectral visions stretched out against the baking pale blue sky did nothing to assist the recovery of my internal functions. Nor did it help my still-shaky legs to negotiate the irregularities of the stony path. Feeling now distinctly giddy, I focused my eyes instead upon the rough track before me as it meandered slowly up the rise through the coastal forest, which became more overgrown the further I advanced.

After several minutes the path emerged onto flatter terrain. The trees fell away mercifully to either side and I found myself emerging onto cleared ground.

Before me was an open, crudely mown lawn, before a two-storied building made from rough bricks and blocks of pale stone. Surrounding this were other, smaller brick and timber buildings stretching away across the clearing, some surrounded by small plots and gardens. These were connected by tracks and pathways, leading away towards clusters of rather meaner shacks across a small gully. Some of these ramshackle shelters appeared to be rudely cobbled together from mere leaves and sticks.

I approached the large stone building uncertainly, walked around the pathway until I found a portal beneath a large sign saying "Government House, HM Colony of Port Fortitude". I rapped cautiously upon what was apparently the front door.

After a moment it was opened by a young servant woman of plainish and rather pinkish appearance.

"Yes?" she inquired brusquely, wiping her hands upon her apron and blowing a strand of sandy hair aside which had loosened itself from her cotton bonnet.

"Oh. I… could I see the Governor, please?"

The girl appeared for a moment unable to answer, mouth half open and eyes wide as she scrutinised uncertainly my still damp and no doubt highly dishevelled form.

Attempting to correct what I admit must have been constituted a fairly poor visual first impression, I cleared my throat and demanded "This is, er, Government House, is it not?"

"It is", she managed through the still gaping mouth.

At this I repeated, rather more slowly and with what I fancied was a suitable note of authority, "Then I wish to see the Governor, if you please."

"Oh, that right? An' who might *you* be?" she demanded in broad Cockney, with another contemptuous up-and-down scanning. "Look like you've been dragged backwards through a mangle, you do."

"Ah. Yes. Indeed," I acknowledged, glancing down at my wretched, emaciated form with an embarrassed grin. "Well, you know… got a bit er, you know, getting ashore. From the, er, the ship." I gestured vaguely back towards the docks.

She waited, still looking suspicious and rather less than co-operative. Clearly, some further reassurance would be needed in order to proceed beyond this obstacle.

"Oh. Ah, I'm Tom," I blurted. She looked utterly blank at this, and realising that my vague and childish informality would cut no mustard whatsoever with her, I spluttered to correct it: "Er, Thomas… er, Quayle."

I took a deep breath and made another attempt. "Dr Thomas Quayle. The... the new surgeon."

"Surgeon?" She echoed, and looked me up and down, one corner of her lip curling upward into her dimpled cheek in palpable disbelief. "You're a *doctor?*" I grinned sheepishly in confirmation.

"Well," she pronounced most decidedly, "you don't look like one."

"Well, indeed I am, er, a doctor," I hastened on, "and not only that, but... er, the..." But she had already closed the door in my face before I could finish, so that I was forced now to shout through the closed portal: "*...the governor's nephew!*"

It was a mere second before the door opened again, just a crack this time, the pink face peering out. "You what?"

"I'm the governor's..." I confirmed with a small embarrassed cough, "nephew" (this with a fixed grin).

"Oh." She appraised me once more, eyes narrowed, considering. Even the slight possibility of such a preposterous claim turning out to be true had clearly changed the state of things; and I must have looked by now as if my patience was wearing rather thin.

Well," she determined at last, "you better come in then."

She opened the door and turned to me. "You wait 'ere." She marched briskly off down a long hallway. I entered slowly, gazing about at the crude stonework of the small foyer, its clay plastering apparently done in a hodge-podge mixture of rich red-brown and silver-grey, its painting by no means completed.

I stood waiting there for several moments until the maidservant reappeared. "All right," she said, still with a slight tone of uncertainty, "come wi' me then."

She led me along the hall and around a corner, where she stopped and indicated a solid-looking door bearing a large brass plaque carrying the legend "SIR HENRY BLYTHE, Governor".

"Knock there an' wait to be called in," she instructed. And with that, off she marched, pausing to cast one more suspicious look over her shoulder, as if to reassure herself that I was not ducking away to help myself to the best silver.

I drew myself up straight, took a deep breath and knocked, rather more tentatively than I had intended.

"Enter!" came the daunting bark from within.

4. THICKER THAN WATER

Entering the commodious room I beheld at its far side my uncle, the Governor – for I knew it must be he, though we had never met. He was seated behind his enormous desk, working on some papers.

To approach him it was necessary to make my way around the large model upon the table in the centre of the room. This I did; I came up to the desk and waited, blinking down at the thinning silvery hair before me.

After what seemed an inordinately long time, he finally deigned to look up, raising his bushy eyebrows to fix his sternly appraising eyes squarely upon me. I could see now the sibling resemblance to my mother – particularly the long-suffering steeliness of the gaze which now fell upon me with considerably less than approval.

I smiled. He did not return the smile, but acknowledged me brusquely: "Ah. Young Quayle. So your ship has come in, as they say." Now it was his turn to eye me up and down with evident disfavour. "If indeed you did come by ship…"

"Oh… yes, Uncle," I began to explain, "I just…. it was the…" I grinned and extended my hand to him, but this was ignored as he rose from behind the desk, drawing himself up the not enormous distance to his full stature, the top of his balding pate coming to just above my shoulder. Appearing to become rather too abruptly aware of the height disparity between us, he motioned me in some irritation towards a large straight-backed chair facing his desk.

"Sit down. Sit." As if to a recalcitrant dog. I hastened to do so. He remaining standing, balanced dramatically upon the balls of both feet, while he launched into what must have been a well practised speech.

"Your ship has indeed come in, as I said – and its name is the HMS Last Chance", he pronounced, with apparent grim satisfaction at the gravity and wit of this. Without waiting for any reaction from me, he began to pace around me as a lion-tamer would around his cowed charge.

"Wasn't easy for me to wangle you this post", he said sternly – adding heavily, "not given your *record…*"

Not wishing this particular subject to be dwelt upon in any uncomfortable detail, I cut in quickly: "Yes, well I must say, uncle, how grateful…"

"Never mind that," he cut me off abruptly, stopping dead in his tracks. "And don't call me 'Uncle' ".

"Sorry, er… Excellency."

"In any case…" waving me aside and resuming his pacing, "…unfortunate death of your predecessor here, Dr Helfcott, provided an opportunity which I, and your good mother, and indeed your entire family, will *thank you not to squander*" (this last utterance delivered with unmistakeably emphatic pauses between the words).

"No, sir." This was a bare squeak, crushed beneath the weight of the mental image of my poor mother's anguished face as she'd half-begged, half-browbeaten me to accept this small straw of a chance to redeem my tarnished image and to do some belated justice to the family's proud naval traditions. Even my terror at the prospect of the long sea voyage, and of what lay beyond it, was never a match for such emotional pressure. All the eloquent pleading, profuse apologising, sincere promising and respectful questioning in the world would never divert such a determined parent.

The whole process had taken almost two years – from Mother's desperate letter sent across the ocean to her brother, through her (and my) anguished wait for a reply, and to the final receipt of a terse missive from Sir Henry to the effect that he had written to the Colonial Office with notice of the appointment and I was free to come out to the colony on the next available ship.

All the while I had clung frantically to the shreds of my career, my weak protestations finally fading to silence before my mother's invocations of the cherished memory of my poor dear father who had perished heroically in a sea battle when I was but a child.

How fervently poor Mother had hoped and expected that her only son would emulate his celebrated father in a distinguished naval career – and how bitterly disappointed she had been in that expectation. When it had first become unavoidably evident that I had precious little affinity for the art of seamanship – and even less for the rigours of battle – I had been deftly shunted into the less hazardous realm of naval surgery. Alas, even there I had proved unequal to the upkeep of the family tradition. The spirit was willing, but the flesh (particularly about the vitals) was alas, weak indeed.

Uncle was now in full stride. He was keen to complete a duty of kinship with which he was clearly impatient. Perhaps in view of my past record he had, it seemed, made a decision to dispense entirely with the kind of warm and sympathetic family welcome I might have expected, almost to the point of waiving politeness altogether. I would be dealt with, it was evident, not as a relative, nor even as a professional, but as a juvenile transgressor facing a severe corrective official.

"This is a straightforward job, Quayle," he continued gruffly, "one that even you ought to be capable of. As you know, there's a private doctor, that is Dr Mountfort, to treat the rest of us – officers, free settlers. You need only to attend to the convicts. Ointments for their poxes, stitches for their stab wounds… most of all, your duty is to keep them fit to work."

At this point he strode to his model, surveying it proudly. "That is what will make this colony grow and prosper, Quayle - work and lots of it."

He turned his back on me, pacing about again as he continued the lecture: "I am determined to make Port Fortitude a great and lasting settlement – and Heaven help the man who stands in the way of that aim. Do I make myself clear?" This last utterly rhetorical utterance was delivered facing me, towering over me – which, given his want of altitude, was only possible with me sitting and he standing.

I am sure I gulped audibly, answering almost in a whisper: "Quite clear, sir. I shall… do the best I can."

This was clearly the wrong response. His eyes narrowed grimly at it. "Mm. Not sure I find that particularly reassuring."

I grinned weakly, as if that would do anything at all to add reassurance. Still ignoring my reactions utterly, he returned to his desk, standing behind it, looking down at his piles of documents.

"Have to say I'd very much rather *not* have to deal with any extra responsibilities at the moment, the business of government here being as demanding as it is. But after all, family is family, and…"

And at this very apposite point the door was flung open with a crash - and an absolute vision burst into the room, as if to personify the ubiquitousness of the family responsibility to which the Governor had just alluded.

"Really, Papa, it's the last straw! It's hopelessly out of tune!"

She stopped, seeing me. She smiled, tossed aside a shining lock of auburn hair and batted her extraordinary eyelashes at me - atop eyes, hazel like her father's, but as large and limpid as tropical pools, as she almost cooed:

"Oh… hello."

The silence was broken first by my gulping several times, then by the Governor's quietly sarcastic, muttered "By all means, *enter.*"

"I've *already* entered, silly," she trilled with a girlish chuckle that washed over me like manna from Heaven.

"Mm, so you have," agreed her father with something less than delight. And then, as if gripped by a momentary attack of the ordinary social niceties: "Felicity, allow me to introduce your cousin - Dr Thomas Quayle."

Felicity. The perfect name for such a vision. She extended her hand langorously towards me and I leapt to my feet, taking it, though not quite sure what exactly to do with it.

"Oh. Y-yes…" I stammered.

"Charmed", she offered, though now eyeing my bedraggled appearance rather more closely, and consequently sounding rather unconvincing in this last utterance.

"Y-yes," I continued to stammer. "Er, you are. I mean, so am I, er… Miss Felicity. Cousin." I was shaking her hand now - perhaps rather too earnestly, since she hurriedly extracted it from my admittedly putrid grasp, still clearly straining to take in how any human being could possibly sink to such a level of physical debasement. I fancy I detected a barely-suppressed sniff or even perhaps a slight gagging.

I was rescued from further embarrassment by my uncle. "Well, *Doctor,*" (this with a firm tone of reminder as to what my sole proper function here was to be), "you'd best be getting to your quarters and smarten yourself up after your voyage. Polly!"

The maidservant re-entered and was instructed: "Send in Major Bascombe, would you."

"Excellency." She bustled off.

Fearing the too rapid loss of an opportunity to converse, however briefly, with my most appealing cousin, I ventured breezily: "I er… play a little piano myself."

"Indeed", she responded politely. And then an idea appeared to occur to her, tilting her delicate head most appealingly towards me as she inquired: "You couldn't… *tune* one, by any chance, could you?"

Honesty reared its noble head only for an instant, before being chased into craven oblivion by the full force of rank opportunism. "Well, I… er, probably." I shrugged nonchalantly at this most flagrant lie – which I compounded with an exaggerated nod of feigned earnestness, as I pledged again: "I shall do the best I can."

At this, my uncle shot me a look of the sharpest iciness – my endurance of which was rendered quite worthwhile by the darling girl batting those wonderful eyelashes at me once more, and smiling at me in the most damnably disarming fashion. "Oh, I should be *ever* so grateful."

I responded with a puppy-like grin as the door was rapped again, the Governor's barked imperative rang out afresh, and a tall uniformed man entered.

"Major Bascombe," barked Blythe by way of formal introduction, "Dr Quayle, our new colonial surgeon."

The said Major had removed his hat smartly to reveal a most impressive set of sideburns, which appeared to be entirely engaged in the difficult business of attempting to buttress the features suspended mournfully between them. His bearing was erect and proper enough, the large chin raised, the eyes fixed directly upon me; but at the same time I fancy I sensed something in the lined and worn face betraying the unmistakeable sag of a man much disappointed in life - the eyes conveying a resignation to what must be, but at the same time the subcutaneous scars of what might have been.

Bascombe immediately joined the procession of people who had run their eyes up and down my waterlogged form in varying degrees of disgust – his perhaps the least disguised of all.

I hastened to shake hands with the Major, but he was at this point occupied in saluting the Governor. I responded to this by raising my own hand in salute to the Major – at the same instant that he lowered his to shake hands with me. It was not an auspicious beginning to our working relationship.

The handshake never consummated, we were interrupted by a loud CRACK! from somewhere outside the window. It was followed by an anguished male scream. Without thinking I raced to the casement and stood before it, gaping in horror at what lay without.

In the square beyond the lawn was a gathering of troopers, convicts and settlers. At the centre a sturdy wooden triangle had been erected, upon which was tied the spreadeagled figure of a man, stripped to the waist. Another man was standing beside him with a large, nasty, multi-stranded whip. And next to him was a smaller, dark-coated, dog-collared figure, evidently a man of the cloth.

As I watched, aghast, the whip was raised and brought down with considerable force against the bare back of the tied man.

CRACK! I could not prevent myself wincing and turning away as the prisoner screamed.

"Oh no, Bascombe," came Blythe's weary voice from beside me. "Not *another* flogging." The Major jutted out his angular chin defensively as the Governor inquired: "What was it for *this* time?"

"Insolence, sir", came the stiff reply, in a provincial accent suggesting an origin among the merchant classes to the northern parts of England, probably Yorkshire.

"What did he call you?" inquired the Governor wearily.

With a sidelong, shifting glance, the Major replied quietly through clenched teeth: "I'd rather not say, sir."

Blythe rolled his eyes. "For Heaven's sake, Bascombe, sticks and stones - look here, if we go on flogging men for every insult, we'll soon have none left to carry out my visionary public works program." And he gestured impatiently towards his model.

CRACK! Again I could not help wincing, even without looking. As I turned back, I fancied I could see the cleric smacking his hand enthusiastically into his fist and smirking. He was muttering something, as if in ritual incantation.

"Yes, but sir," protested the Major, "you know these Irish. Rebellious scum, the lot of 'em. Give 'em an inch and they'll be…"

The Governor had apparently heard this often and finished the well-known prognostication in sing-song fashion: "… murdering us in our beds! Yes, well I don't think they'll be overthrowing the British Empire by calling us rude names, Bascombe." He peered out the window. I had turned away and was attempting to think of almost anything else, my vitals in turmoil.

CRACK!

Blythe turned from the flogging with annoyance. "Look, I can't think, let alone work, with that racket going on. Go out and put a stop to it, Bascombe. And for God's sake, don't say you'll 'do the best you can'."

The chin quivered. "I shall do my best not to, sir."

The Governor looked daggers at him before adding: "And show Dr Quayle here to his quarters."

Bascombe saluted and headed briskly for the door. I realised I was expected to follow without further ado, and hastened to follow him. My uncle shouted after us: "And he'll need a horse!"

I followed the Major as he strode down the hallway, out of the door, down the path and out onto the square. As we emerged into the roadway there was another CRACK! and a loud scream, trailing off into the most awful moan.

We came up behind the squirming cleric, who I now heard was muttering something about "The Lord's justice" and "a tooth for a tooth" as he pounded his fist with repressed violence into his chubby palm. He turned to face Bascombe, who barked out to the other officers:

"All right, that's enough. Cut him down." The soldiers moved to do the Major's bidding, the poor prisoner slumping to the ground, his bloodied back a ghastly mess. I felt my insides rising to the occasion.

The minister looked scandalised, his pudgy features stretching into a resentful pout as he protested in the manner of a child denied a toy: "But he's only had 37 !"

"Governor's orders, Reverend," said Bascombe sharply. "Doesn't want his… public works jeopardised." This with the slight suggestion of a sneer.

"We are treating these Popish scoundrels too leniently altogether," murmured the chaplain darkly. "And I fear we do so at our peril. In no time they will be overrunning us."

"Aye - murdering us in our beds", agreed the Major.

"Do you know, they are even allowing the Catholics to send their priests to the colonies, to lure the convicts away from the Holy Church of England? Well, what in Heaven must we endure next?" Reverend Staines threw up his hands in horror at the prospect of such unthinkable competition.

I meanwhile ignored the protestations of my heaving entrails and bent to attend to the wretched prisoner, who was babbling incoherently. I had witnessed several floggings aboard various ships, but none as ferocious as this.

"My God," I blurted, "the poor man's half dead! Here, let me have a look at him." I drew back at the sight of his back, criss-crossed with the most dreadful bleeding weals. "Oh, good God!" I felt the tumult within my vitals rising to thwart my endeavours, but fought it back.

I crouched to the harrowing task. Behind me I overheard the hushed tones of the Reverend, aside to the Major: "Oh dear, we've got another soft one, have we?"

"Aye," came the whispered reply. "And he's the Governor's nephew."

"Merciful Heaven preserve us."

5. SHAMELESS

I can remember little of what transpired immediately after this, my mind blotting most of the gory details from my memory as it had so often been necessary to do during my inauspicious career. My next recollection is that some time later, after I had apparently done what I could for the unfortunate convict, Bascombe and I had repaired to the barracks – where the Major was now guiding me around that establishment.

I was introduced perfunctorily to some of the subordinate officers, an assortment of callow and mostly gormless young fellows with unnecessarily strong handshakes. Apart from the uniforms, the singular common feature I ascertained in all of the officers was that they all smelled quite distinctly of rum.

Major Bascombe's second-in-command at the barracks was Captain John Partridge, an affable, smiling, babyfaced fellow, almost the antithesis of his sullen superior. Partridge greeted me quite cheerfully, saying I should feel free to come to him for any necessary assistance as the need arose. Bascombe appeared irritated at such pleasantries, cutting the Captain off rather rudely and ushering me impatiently onwards to acquaint me with the barracks.

I was shunted into a small room. "Your quarters are in here," said the Major. "More modest than what *you're* used to, I'll warrant, but…"

I entered my new abode, throwing my salt-caked and now blood-spattered coat upon the single chair.

I looked about. Yes, it was basic indeed, of rude timber construction, with visible gaps in the walls, but it had at least a good firm bed – and more importantly, good firm fixed earth beneath it.

"I'm sure it will be entirely adequate," I concluded, "just as long as the floor remains horizontal." I grinned in a weak attempt to somehow break the ice with my surly new colleague.

The Major merely grunted. Giving up on the icebreaking for the moment, I cast my eye about the room in search of my luggage, which I had presumed would have been brought to my quarters by now. "Oh, er… my trunk," I inquired, "where has it been put?"

A blank look from Bascombe. "Trunk, Doctor?"

"My trunk, yes. I entrusted it to a man down at the beach. He was standing against… a post…"

"A man?" His eyes narrowed sharply. "And did this man happen to have… *arrows* on his shirt?"

"Well, yes, now that you mention it, he…"

But there was no point continuing. I trailed off hopelessly into the most profound misgivings as a fierce sneer spread over the jutting features of the Major. He shook his head, the large chin quivering in loathing.

"A convict," he spat. "Those that aren't thieves are robbers. You see his face?"

"Well, no, not really, It was covered by a… hat."

"Nothing to be done, I'm afraid", he pronounced. "That'll be the last you'll see of your trunk, I daresay."

I was aghast at this. "But… but it has my instruments… my clothes…."

He sniffed. "Nothing to be done", he repeated. "Put it down to *bitter experience.*" This with the bleakly irrefutable authority of one whose experience had consisted almost entirely of bitterness, or had at least been interpreted as such.

"But…"

He would brook no further buts and ignored me, heading out the door and off along the short corridor with a barked "Come on."

I was left no choice but to trail in his wake, he continuing to point out relevant areas of my working and living space. "Along here is your surgery… and further along is the commander's office. You'll find me in there more often than not…"

This was a surprise. "Oh, I thought… Colonel McMurdough was the commanding officer here."

He gritted his teeth, sidelevers bristling and chin quivering anew at the mention of this name. "Colonel McMurdough", he clarified through clenched teeth, "is indeed our 'commander', in name at least. But you'll not find *him* round here too often – too busy tending to his *flock.*" He cast a contemptuous glance out the window.

"What, he's a clergyman as well as… ?"

"No," he grimaced mirthlessly, "slightly less intelligent flock. Slightly. Sheep. The Colonel is a *great pastoralist.* Spends most of his precious time stocking up his magnificent property. Leaving *me* doing the real work of running the regiment, *and,"* he added with a fresh sneer, "also tending to the Governor's *paperwork.*"

Now the chin was at maximum quiver, the suppressed bitterness reaching its zenith at the mention of this duty. "To get the plum pickings", he concluded with an accusing look directly at me, "it appears you must come from the right family. Us career soldiers must compete for the scraps."

I knew not how I could respond to this, nor indeed which way to look. He paused, then mercifully ended the awkward moment by taking a deep breath and then uttering mournfully, as if pronouncing an unpleasant sentence of punishment: "Speaking of which, we'd best get down to see *Halloran."* And with this he turned towards the door with his usual dreary finality.

"Ah. Yes," I responded uncertainly, this name ringing no bells with me. I followed obediently at the Major's heel, out of the barracks and along the pathway towards a long, low, ragged-looking building, apparently the stables.

After a moment I dared to ask: "Er, who is… Halloran?"

"Stablehand," he answered with a fresh sneer. "Seamus Halloran, by name, but 'Shameless' they call him – and with good reason." He sniffed with derision. "Irishman. Convict of course. Ticket-of-leave man."

"Ah yes, ticket-of-leave," I said, eager to appear to know at least something of life in the colony. "So if I understand the system, he's earned a limited freedom and a degree of trust in return for… good behaviour?"

He sneered with unadulterated scorn. "In his case, in return for several years of *undetected crime."*

Inside the stables, the aforementioned Seamus "Shameless" Halloran is busy. Engaged in the keen examination of an elegant snuffbox, while he polishes it with a grimy cloth. With one calloused hand he rubs his well-stubbled chin and assesses the small treasure, turning it over to check for any defects that might impact adversely on the sale price.

Not bad, he thinks, not bad at all. Good condition, especially considerin' its long voyage. Yes, he concludes to himself, that little beauty should fetch a good tradeable quantity of rum.

Coinage being scarce in the fledgling settlement, and mineral extraction as yet a mere vision, "rum" (a generic term hereabouts for any alcoholic spirit) has become the main currency. It possesses the essential feature of any currency: it adheres to the basic laws of supply and demand.

On the supply side, real rum could only be made from sugarcane, not yet grown here in Port Fortitude. In the early years, indeed, not much grain at all was able to take root in the colony's swampy, sandy soils. This meant that a few years back, the enterprising troopers were able to buy up all the supplies of corn-mash gin on a trader from the West Indies, and thus secure a virtual monopoly on this fluid currency. They then reaped a small fortune by selling it at a substantial profit to the free settlers and (with one S. Halloran reaping a tidy commission as intermediary) to the ticket-of-leave convicts.

But now more supplies have arrived, and the settlement has begun to spread westward into more fertile lands towards the mountains, and to grow its own crops on a more substantial scale. The monopoly has been eased and the alcoholic currency has become less narrowly controlled.

Now to the demand side. This is well assured by the profusion of trials, tribulations, fears, doubts and disappointments suffered by settlers, soldiers and convicts, from which the prospect of at least temporary escape into sweet oblivion is all too attractive. Cowrie shells may be appealing - but they just don't cut it in the currency stakes alongside such potent stuff.

But of course that's also the downside of this currency: while coins or tokens tend to be saved and stored for future use in buying clothes, food or other supplies, rum has a definite tendency, on being acquired, to be rather too rapidly consumed. This leads to all sorts of undesirable and problematic behaviour, ranging from violence and disorder to simply staggering, falling over or refusing to rise in the morning. And that's just its effect on the troopers — the convicts are even worse.

All in all, the prevalence of such currency does little to foster behaviours conducive to efficient trade and commerce or to the rapid development of a vigorous, dynamic settlement.

Still, things be as they be, thinks Shameless Halloran — who is nothing if not a man of philosophical mind, and more adept than most at taking life as it comes and making the best of it. He examines the snuffbox one last time and licks his lips, savouring the prospect of both saving and consuming - in moderation, he tells himself, being a man of moderation, he tells himself - the significant volume of liquid currency for which he hopes this little piece might be traded.

But now he looks up with a start, eyes darting and each ragged hair on the fleshy ears, along with the ears themselves, almost visibly pricking up. Hearing noises approaching outside, he hurriedly replaces the snuffbox among some medicinal-looking bottles on a shelf. Slides this back into a hidden panel in the wall and locks it into place with a reassuring click. Pulls a saddlecloth over the panel. Admires the resulting disappearance with satisfaction.

There you go, me little nest-egg, he thinks — all nice and snug.

He hitches up his belt and rolls up his sleeves as he hastens outside in response to a sharp and unpleasantly familiar voice — a voice he has learned from painful experience must not be long trifled with.

"Halloran!" barked Bascombe as we drew up in front of the stables. There was no immediate response to this, so he repeated more loudly:

"*Halloran!*" And for good measure, "Get your lazy bog-Irish arse out here at once!"

At this pleasant imprecation, a rather pot-bellied fellow of indeterminately middle age, dressed in shabby arrow-headed garb, emerged from the stables - prattling in an almost theatrical Irish brogue like some captured pantomime leprechaun about to grant a wish: "Here I am, sir, at your service. Sure an' it's a lovely mornin'! What can I be doin' for you two good gentlemen?"

"Cut the paddy palaver, Halloran," snapped the Major. "Dr Quayle here" (with a perfunctory nod at me) "is our new colonial surgeon. He'll be needing a horse. A good one, mind, not your usual nags."

"Ah, delighted to meet you, doctor," said the smiling stablehand, turning towards me. At once I felt that the crinkled, weatherworn visage and the jovial Irish accent were somewhat familiar. I looked at him more closely as he grinned and gestured, his pupils darting about like deranged mosquitoes trying to escape from his head, his genial patter rattling onward:

"Welcome to Port Fortitude. I'll be gettin' you saddled up then, sir - since I am as you might say, *saddled* with that responsibility (ha ha)!" His mobile, fleshy face creased readily into an enormous grin as he chuckled at his own rather weak jape.

Bascombe, clearly at the end of his patience – which, it could be assumed, did not extend far at the best of times with regard to this Irishman - rolled his eyes and snarled icily at him: "Shut up and get *on* with it."

"Right you are, sir." The stablehand, having decided he had pushed the cheery prattle as far as he dared, bowed his head and turned to obey - but I stopped him, now remembering more definitely the moment of my arrival upon the beach and the encounter with the arrowhead-garbed fellow under the straw hat.

"I say… haven't we already met?"

He turned to me with a look of convincing bewilderment, blinking like a startled animal caught in the beam of a lantern. "I… don't believe I've had the pleasure, sir."

"I left my trunk in your care, didn't I?"

His response came like lightning, the eyes barely flickering. "Us convicts all look the same, sir. It's the tailorin'." A wink and another chuckle at this – but it was immediately transformed into a startled cry and a gasp for breath, as Bascombe stepped forward, seized him roughly by the shirt collar and twisted it, raising the poor fellow onto his tip-toes.

"You thieving scoundrel!" growled the Major. "What have you done with the doctor's trunk?"

"It wasn't me, sir," squawked the convict, dangling like a portly marionette, his feet scraping dustily for purchase. "I was never down at the beach this mornin'."

"We'll soon find out," snarled Bascombe with venom. "A good *flogging* ought to get the truth out of him." At this, the Major released his hold on the stablehand, who slumped wheezing and gasping to the ground. "I'll have it arranged right away. Nothing a few strokes of the lash won't...."

Perhaps it was the prospect of having to witness another of those dreadful spectacles, and worse, to attend to its gory aftermath. In any case, the immediate churning in my vitals propelled me toward immediate interruption. Certainly there was more gut than brains in the decision.

"No!" I blurted.

There was a moment's pause. Bascombe turned to me, teeth clenched. "*What?*"

"It... wasn't him," I said, less than convincingly. The Major certainly did not appear convinced – indeed he stood with mouth agape, apparently unable to believe his ears, merely repeating: "*What* are you saying?"

"I was... mistaken", I persisted. "The man on the beach was... was much taller. And..." I was thinking quickly now, "... he, er... walked with a pronounced limp."

Bascombe considered this for an instant, eyes narrowed. "From what you told me, he never moved. Standing against a post, you said."

"Well, he er...he... stood with a limp." I smiled weakly at him, appalled that this was the best I could come up with.

The Major took a deep breath, then grasped my arm firmly and led me aside, growling in a stage whisper: "Listen, don't let these people get the better of you, Doctor. I keep telling the Governor – too much of this soft treatment, this 'rehabilitation' he goes on about, and they'll be murdering us in our beds..."

"This isn't the man," I repeated simply and stubbornly, meeting his gaze as directly as I could manage.

Bascombe looked positively fierce, his prominent chin quivering intensely. I almost imagined he was about to seize me by the scruff of the neck and dangle me aloft in the same brutal manner as he had manhandled the hated Irishman. After a moment, however, he appeared to suppress his rage, released my arm with a contemptuous sniff, and said very quietly:

"As you wish, doctor. Be it on your own head. I'll see you back at the barracks." And after a last hateful grimace at the still-seated ticket-of-leaver who had so heinously escaped his just punishment for yet another undetected crime, the Major turned on his heel and strode grimly off towards the barracks compound, a cloud of dust trailing behind him.

I turned and extended my hand towards the half-prostrate Halloran, who took it and allowed me to assist him shakily to his feet.

"Thank you very kindly, Your Doctorship," he said meekly, making a rudimentary effort at dusting himself off while rubbing his chafed neck. "I'm most grateful to you."

"Well," I responded, not wishing to appear too easy a mark, *"I'd* be grateful to get my *trunk* back." I looked at him sternly.

He appeared chastened, responding earnestly: "I'll move heaven and earth to see that it... er, turns up, sir."

"As long as it 'turns up' by no later than tomorrow, I shall say no more."

"Don't you worry, doctor, I'll...." But he trailed off, gaping over my shoulder at the sight of something behind me. I heard a familiar slow thudding of approaching hooves, and turned to see what was arriving; as Halloran, mouth dropping open almost to his boots, gasped: *"Holy Mother!"*

6. GREAT EXPLORATIONS

Approaching us was the bizarre and imposing form of the camel I had seen earlier on the beach, with its same bearded and pith-helmeted master still atop, and native hand beside.

Halloran took a faltering step towards the strange party, open-mouthed and blinking in astonishment.

The camel lurched to a halt before us and its rider slid rather awkwardly to the ground, lurching for a moment as if about to fall. At closer quarters now I could see that, though very wild and unkempt, he was much younger than I had first imagined – quite a young chap, in fact.

He straightened up, dusted himself off and announced in his high-born and stentorian lisp: "Captain Maximilian Ffeffington-Weekes, Explorer to His Majesty." Then, casting his intense blue eyes with some disgust towards the dilapidated premises behind us, he demanded: "Are you in charge of these…" (he clearly hesitated to use the word) "… stables?"

Mistaking me for a stablehand was not an unreasonable mistake, since I was still wearing my putrid and bedraggled sea-voyage attire - towards which (why was I no longer surprised at this reaction?) the explorer now flung an even more disgusted look.

"Er, not really," I hastened to correct him, " I'm er…"

But the haughty helmeted one was not the least interested in anything at all that I might have to say upon the matter, steaming on in grand imperviousness: "Make sure this beast is well cared for, it has just endured an expedition of epic proportions. And…" (lowering his voice slightly as he indicated the smiling native) "… keep your eye on 'Jacky' here. I believe he can be trusted, but you never know with natives." He narrowed his eyes at this, as if suddenly watchful for a sneak attack.

I glanced at the said native, who appeared to be taking no notice of this, his dark eyes fixed vaguely upon a point somewhere in the middle distance.

"Oh, don't worry about him overhearing," said Ffeffington-Weekes with a contemptuous gesture towards him, "he can't understand us, doesn't speak a word of English. Apart from the few rudimentary commands I have endeavoured to teach him, and despite my Christian civilising influence, he remains essentially an ignorant savage."

I gave a gesture of non-committal acknowledgment.

Halloran, meanwhile, was still staring at the camel. He at last pronounced with vigour: "Sure an' that's the funniest-lookin' horse I've ever seen."

The explorer snorted with contempt as he corrected this: "Camel."

"You what, sir?"

The Captain articulated with exaggeration as if teaching a child to speak: "*Cah-mell.*"

"Ah," said the stablehand, nodding slowly as he took this in. Then he turned back to the beast: "Well... *Carmel,* you're the funniest-lookin' horse I've ever seen."

Ffeffington-Weekes rolled his eyes in utter contempt at this, and without another word swept off on foot towards Government House – leaving Jacky to lead the camel into the stables, Halloran gawping along behind. As the native camel-hand disappeared within, he half-turned and slipped me what I must surely have imagined was half a wink.

In her childishly-decorated Government House bedchamber, Felicity Blythe is having her hair done by Polly, whose pink but work-toughened hands skilfully forge elaborate plaits in the gorgeous silken tresses of the Governor's daughter.

Having spent the past two hours painstakingly brushing, folding and hanging vast quantities of fashionable new clothes recently unloaded from the ship, under the impatient and impulsive direction of her youthful mistress, Polly's in no mood to perform her present task. But perform it she must. The maidservant is fortunately standing behind her mistress, her face above the reflection of the mirror, so Felicity is not in a position to see the young convict woman's expressions while carrying out the intricate hairdressing. This is a good thing – since these expressions are less than enthusiastic. Though this labour is undoubtedly much less physically onerous than lugging washing or feeding pigs, it does involve enduring young Milady's conversation – which to Polly, leaves rather a lot to be desired.

"Well at last, a bit of excitement around here," trills Felicity, beaming. "There's to be a proper banquet, of course, in honour of his return."

"Whose, Milady?" asks Polly politely.

"Captain Ffeffington-Weekes, silly. Explorer of the Great Interior, discoverer of the massive Inland Sea. And he's quite gorgeously handsome… and," she adds perhaps most enthusiastically, "he comes from a particularly wealthy family. I must get to know him better," she concludes.

The maidservant's tone is flat, controlled. "I'm sure you will, Milady. I'm sure you will."

Felicity doesn't notice the sarcasm. Her one thought: how to home in on this eligible bachelor with all due speed.

"At long last!" she exclaims. "A young man of suitable breeding and appearance! Indeed, the only decent prospect I have encountered in almost a year in this blasted backwater, since Papa dragged me out here on the promise of its 'great prospects for rapid social advancement'. Great prospects indeed! A mere handful of landed settlers, every man of them either already married or else positively moribund!"

She pouts irritably. "I am sure Papa only brought me here because with Mother so long dead he needed someone to handle his social arrangements. Well, rest assured, I shall make the most of this rare opportunity. Papa has promised me I shall play the piano at the banquet," she beams; and then adds dismissively, "as soon as that wet chap has tuned it up."

Polly is faintly appalled at this. "'Wet chap?' You mean your cousin, Dr Quayle?"

"Yes, yes, him" says Felicity with impatience, flapping her hand as if brushing flies away.

" 'e seems rather taken with you," observes Polly, *thinking to herself: quite a good lookin' feller, too, that young doctor, though he certainly was rather wet – smelled a bit off, too. Still, long sea voyage can be a bit of a trial. She chuckles to herself. I think I gave him rather a hard time at the door, when he first turned up. Did look more like a drowned rat than a doctor, though. Still, not so bad – eyes maybe a bit close together, nose maybe a bit big, certainly needs a good haircut, but for all that, a kindness in the face...*

"Yes, well I hope he hurries up with the tuning," snaps Felicity, interrupting her servant's train of thought. *Now,"* she puts her forefinger thoughtfully to her chin, "what should I wear, to drive the great explorer quite mad?"

It is yet another utterance not requiring a response from Polly, who mutters to herself unheard by her mistress: "Bit late for that, from what I hear."

The Great Explorer himself, meanwhile, is recovering from his arduous mission, ensconced within his quarters at the barracks. He's insisted upon his own room, and at the Governor's direction, three of the junior officers have been forced to cram into a shared room in order that the adventurous Captain's demand for a private chamber can be met. The room has been scrubbed and swept by several hastily conscripted convicts in readiness for his occupancy.

Washed and dressed now in a crisp fresh white shirt, the heroic one stands before his full-length mirror, trimming his ginger beard with an exaggerated flourish.

He pauses and turns his face slightly, apparently well pleased with the results of his grooming. You handsome devil, *he thinks, with a cavalier toss of his now shining bronze locks.*

He begins to strike poses of noble bearing – but finds this difficult, as it requires mostly a profile aspect and he cannot at the same time admire himself directly in the glass. He resorts to an elaborate process of first striking the heroic profile pose and then darting a glance at the mirror, hoping to be quick enough to catch the side-on image. No matter how hard he tries, it can't be done. This is a conclusion reached by most children at an early age. Ffeffington-Weekes is still struggling to come to terms with it.

He frowns in frustration at his reflection. Ah, now that looks impressive, *he nods, trying the frown again.* Yes, *he determines,* that is a most successful expression, very commanding. I must use that for appropriate dramatic effect.

He smirks at his reflection, thinking: I expect I shall be quite a hit with the ladies. As usual.

A long queue of shabbily dressed convict patients extended from my external surgery door along the dusty pathway outside. There were scruffy men, sweaty women clutching bawling infants, children – the afflicted protesting their ailments, the able-bodied arguing and fighting. The line seemed endless.

They were indeed mostly, in fact overwhelmingly, Irish – a Hibernian highway of O'Shaughnessys, O'Reillys, O'Herlihys, McGuinnesses, McLaughlins and Megarritys – interrupted only by the occasional Smith or other Cockney.

Inside the surgery itself, it was baking hot – as appeared to be almost routinely the case in the colony. Its enervating heat was relieved only by ferocious sub-tropical storms. If this was a "temperate" climate, I thought, then I would surely dread to experience an "intemperate" one. I had to admit I was almost missing a decent spot of English drizzle - at least one knew what to expect.

I bade farewell to yet another in the procession of convicts who departed from my ministrations carrying small bottles of liquid to be applied to a medical rogues' gallery of minor injuries and infections. I sat back behind the desk, turning to replace a bottle of "Pox Ointment" beside others marked "Purge", "Mercury" and "Medicinal Spirit".

Resting my exhausted limbs for a moment, I reminded myself that I should really count my blessings at this juncture: at least I was now working upon dry land, and feeling rather more healthy with every meal I had managed to keep down. I could almost feel the flesh returning to my bones.

Buoyed somewhat by these thoughts, I took a deep breath and called out "Next please!"

The door opened and I performed a double-take as the next patient entered. It was yet another Irishman – but no ordinary Irishman. This was a familiar, scruffy, pot-bellied figure, who shuffled in rather awkwardly and waddled his way towards me looking less than entirely pleased with the world and his place within it.

"Ah, Halloran," I greeted him.

"Your Doctorship," he responded – not in his earlier lively leprechaun lilt but in much more subdued fashion, with an attempted smile of heroic endurance which emerged more as a grimace. Despite his obvious discomfort, however, I noticed his eyes darting about the room, as if taking in every detail of it within a moment of entering.

"I hope you're here to tell me you've… located my trunk?" I ventured hopefully.

He looked uneasy, eyes dropping. "Well, sir, not exactly…" and then he added, to forestall my frown and the expected reminder of what he had promised: "er, that is to say, there has been definite progress, doctor, definite progress - we're almost there, sir… there are some minor complications, but I'm on the case, sir, well on the case, very confident of havin' it nailed down by er… by…"

"By tomorrow", I cut him off sternly, not to be deprived of my reminder. "You promised. Tomorrow at the latest."

"Tomorrow it is, sir," he agreed meekly, "you can count on it." Then he gave another grimace – one that did not, I fancied, arise entirely from his discomfort at being held to his undertaking.

I prompted: "By the look of you, you're also here for a… medical reason…?" He nodded meekly.

"Well, sit yourself down", I bade him.

He glanced apprehensively at the chair. "If it's… all the same to you, sir, I'd… rather not." At this he gestured vaguely towards his ample posterior.

"Oh. Some… problem astern, eh? Well…" I rose reluctantly, "I suppose the Hippocratic Oath obliges me to at least… have a look?" Another weak grimace from the patient.

"Well, drop them then."

He did so, and I bent to examine the problem. Oh dear, it did not look pleasant. I straightened up, subconsciously suppressing the familiar pang of nausea.

"Mmm, nasty. Some kind of... bite." I bent again to continue the examination. "Horse, was it?"

"No, well, er..." he began haltingly, with some embarrassment, "you see, it was... that Carmel, sir. We didn't see eye to eye."

I looked up from the problem area. "From here, that's obvious. Well," I concluded, straightening again, "this needs stitching. Just a few." He looked now most apprehensive indeed as I reached for a bottle of numbing ointment, which I dabbed onto the offending place, then took needle and thread, and gritting my teeth, began the repair.

He roared with pain. "*Aarrgh!* You have the same gentle touch as your misfortunate predecessor!"

"How do you mean, 'misfortunate'?" I inquired, and wondered aloud: "If indeed there *is* such a word."

He ignored the grammatical query and stuck to the point – as, in a manner of speaking, he was also stuck by it. "A good man, Dr Helfcott. *Owww!* Merciful Mother!"

I chided him gently: "Come now, don't make such a fuss, man. It will be over soon. Here – " (I handed him a scrap of clean dressing) "- bite on this."

He did so and I went on with the dabbing and stitching – continuing the conversation as I did so, partly to occupy both our minds: "So er, what... happened to Dr Helfcott? Some kind of... accident, was it not?"

His voice was muffled by the cloth. "Welh, er, tho it theemed. Came off his horth, thir, thtraight over Thouth 'ead Quiff."

"Where?"

"Thouth 'ead... *owww!*" The cloth dropped from his mouth. "Off South Head Cliff, sir. Straight over. Saved from a watery grave only by the intervention o' the rocks at the bottom. *Owww!*"

"Unfortunate indeed," I agreed, straightening up, the few stitches now completed. "Well, that's about all we can do for you at the moment, Halloran," I said as I placed a small dressing over the repair. "Should do the trick, I think." He gingerly pulled up his trousers, looking extremely sorry for himself.

"We should be able to remove those stitches in about a week," I informed him. "In the meantime, you'd best try not to, er... lean too hard against any posts", I advised him pointedly. His eyes narrowed slightly – and, I fancied, guiltily, at this reference to that first moment upon the beach.

"Thank you, doctor, I'm… indebted to you sir," he mumbled, with something short of full enthusiasm.

I had a thought now, and stopped him as he turned towards the door. "Oh, er, before you go, I… don't suppose you might know of anyone who would have some idea how to… tune a piano, would you?"

At this, the slight twinkle returned to his watery eyes. "Well… we Irish are a very musical people, sir. But it's hard to get the musical muse when a man's in so much pain…"

And with this, his keen eyes darted to a shelf within my open cupboard. "I don't suppose you could spare a small nip o' that…" he indicated a small spirit bottle… "French painkiller? Purely for medicinal purposes, you understand," he added hastily.

I gave him my most disapproving look. "I'm a doctor, Halloran, not an innkeeper."

The twinkle was back in spades now, the pupils dancing about, doing their mosquito jig once more. "Well, nobody's perfect, sir," he said with an impish grin.

I could not prevent a small flicker of a smile coming to my own face as I turned to the cupboard and reached for the bottle.

7. POWER AND POSITION

In the balmy late night breeze, the wheezy swing of a small red-tinted lantern. It tosses its feeble and intermittent blessing hopefully towards a doorway in a moderately-sized but rickety-looking timber shack. This modest edifice is tucked away in a corner of bushland set slightly apart from the main cluster of buildings. Well away from, and decently out of sight of, Government House.

Also swinging in the breeze, suspended from a post above the door, is a rough-hewn timber sign featuring a crude representation of the grinning, rouge-smeared, lipstick-daubed face of a large pointy-snouted fish.

Above the picture in gaudy red letters, the painted words "MARLIN ROUGE."

The Oldest Profession on Earth is well established in Port Fortitude. Official tolerance of it is such that it even gets to hang up its banner - beneath which, the door creaks open and sounds of laughter and merriment are heard from within the Marlin Rouge. Partly visible through its open door, a lurid glow spills out into the night; and spilling out along with it, a well-recognisable figure: jowly, stubbled, clerical collar askew. The figure chortles as it stumbles shakily over the threshold, "Now now, go on with you, no more of your temptations now, you little vixen!" *- as it shakes off the playful grasp of a buxom corseted wench.*

The Reverend Staines looks furtively about, wipes his mouth and adjusts his garments, tugging at the collar in his idiosyncratic fashion. Then he adjusts his bulk into some kind of approximate spheroid equilibrium and slinks none too steadily off into the night.

As he does so, he starts warbling a distinctly slurred rendition of another of Newton's popular – and in the circumstances, disturbingly ironical, Olney Hymns.

Even at his peak, irony would not be the Reverend's strong suit. In his current state, it's not even in the deck. Still, we can appreciate, even if he can't, the suggestive possibilities of a title like "Now Let Us Join with Hearts and Tongues". He burbles:

> *Now let us join with hearts and tongues,*
> *And emulate the angels' songs;*
> *Yea, sinners may address their King*
> *In songs that angels cannot sing…*

Back at the doorway the chaplain's fellow sinner waves in farewell, adjusts her attire matter-of-factly and goes back inside. As the cleric's badly oiled gate creaks its way off into the shadows, the door closes.

And somewhere nearby, an unnoticed watcher melts quietly back into the darkness.

Mosquitoes buzz langorously around the crimson lantern. Night gives way slowly but inexorably to the familiar bright dawn.

Some hours later and some distance away, in the rolling hills well to the west of the harbour, between patches of partly cleared pale green pasture dotted with sheep, a fine horse and cart come hurtling around a track and pull up in a cloud of dust.

Ahead is a surprisingly impressive arched gateway before a grand-looking farmhouse of fairly recent construction, in bricks and solid timber. The dust clears to reveal, seated on the cart, the figures of Colonel Montague McMurdough and his wife Anastasia, both dressed to the nines as usual. In front of them, their convict driver draws lazily at the reins.

A moment's pause. McMurdough gazes through the slowly settling particles towards his rapidly spreading farmlands. Admires the rows of felled trees lying like an elephant graveyard around the expanding perimeters of his sprawling pastures. Imagines, not for the first time, a great empire of totally cleared sheep-strewn farmland stretching to the distant mountains and beyond.

"Well?" snaps the lady, breaking her husband's reverie.

He blinks and turns to her, removing his hat to reveal a surprisingly luxuriant thatch of dark hair. A small curl protrudes down over the broad forehead – a curl deliberately cultivated by his wife because it reminds her of France's rather dashing young rising star, General Bonaparte (when she has mentioned this, her husband has responded stuffily with a disgusted "What – that <u>Frenchman</u>?").

The Colonel now returns his wife's impatient glare with an expression of bewildered blankness. "Well... er, what, my dear?"

"The gate!" *she barks with annoyance. Flaps gloved fingers towards it. My God, she thinks, if brains were fertiliser he would not have such hair.*

"Ah", *he says, with incrementally comprehending nod.* "Yes, of course, my dear." *And turns to the driver, attempting but not really succeeding in matching his wife's level of imperious impatience:* "Well come on, man. Don't just sit there. Open the er, the blasted gate!"

The driver, face impassively unconcerned, slides down in relaxed fashion to do so.

"Tell him to hurry," *snaps Anastasia.* "We do not have all day."

"Yes, dear," *he replies, and again to the driver:* "Er, hurry up there man, we do not have all day!" *– as*

his wife adds, heavenward through clenched teeth: " God, where do we get these people from?"

McMurdough turns back to her, providing the dutifully informative response he understands as being sought: "Well, from here, in the colony, dear. They're convicts." *And he smiles at her, pleased at having explained the situation with such clarity.*

This is returned with some annoyance. She flares: "I <u>know</u> they're... it was a <u>rhetorical</u>..." *Words fail her as they have so many times in dealing with this... with what is referred to as a "husband". Whatever, she wonders as the cart moves through the gate and stops just beyond it, did I see in him?*

"Well?" *she prompts through gritted teeth, angular jaw set, as in her mind's eye sands tumble by the desertload through cosmic hourglasses.*

"Well... er, what, my dear?"

"The gate!" *she almost screams.* "Tell him to shut the gate – and be quick about it!"

"Ah, yes. Quite so," he agrees wisely, and calls out again to the driver, who is already climbing down to shut the gate behind them: *"Shut the gate, man. And be quick about it!"*

The driver, having by now done so, remounts, face impassively unperturbed as if long used to this routine, which indeed he is.

"Move on," commands the Colonel superfluously, the driver having pre-empted him by giving the reins a leisurely shake. *The cart rattles off, carrying its grand pastoral couple up the path to their newly established rural seat.*

Elsewhere, other hooves are drawing slowly up.

Bascombe and I had spent a good three hours scuttling on horseback about the inner reaches of the settlement, inspecting various works in progress.

I had the distinct impression that the Major would have preferred to avoid this duty; indeed, Captain Partridge told me later that Bascombe had referred to it scornfully as "babysitting" and had tried to foist it onto him; but the affable Partridge, though himself not at all unwilling to oblige, was already committed to some work connected with supervision of one of the Governor's building projects – and such activity, the Major knew from *bitter experience,* was to be regarded as being of the highest priority.

The convicts of Port Fortitude were engaged mostly upon the growing of crops, upon the tending of farm animals, and especially upon the construction of buildings, roads and bridges. As we proceeded about our inspection of these last-mentioned works, the Major provided his usual curt and derogatory explanations and comments upon them – describing them variously as "grand", "elaborate", "lengthy", or "of precious little practical value, as far as I can see".

He waited impatiently while I checked the state of health of the convict workers and attended to occasional cases of minor injuries, heat fatigue or other conditions – all of them dismissed by Bascombe in muttered asides as varieties of deliberate malingering. He was quick to allude to the criminal history of each of these workers, often loudly and within their hearing, and usually culminating in summations along the lines of "Honest as the day is night", or "He'd steal anything that wasn't nailed down", or "Not safe to turn your back on under any conditions." I responded non-committally and went about my doctoring work, which would on the whole have been a great deal less burdensome without such unrelentingly negative commentary.

Our tour of duty now completed, our horses lurched mercifully to a stop before the barracks. I slid from the saddle in some discomfort, adjusting the rear of my trousers. Bascombe slipped smoothly from his own saddle as I reached wincing under the girth to undo the strap.

He flung a sharp glance across at me. "What's the matter, Quayle?"

"Oh… nothing," I lied.

We lifted our saddles free and started to walk towards the stables. Or rather, he walked; I waddled. Bascombe peered disapprovingly over at my burden.

"That saddle's much too wide," he pronounced. "Either that or you're too narrow. One or t'other." He shook his head wearily. "I shall have…" (with a sneer) "… *Halloran* find you another."

"No," I said hastily, not wishing to witness another unpleasant confrontation. "No, I am obliged to you, Major, but I believe I can… handle it myself. If you don't mind. Thank you."

"After all this time," he droned, shaking his head, "you'd think he'd have learned to match an arse to a saddle size."

"Hmm," I opined, in what had already become a routine practice of choosing a carefully non-committal path in what I hesitated to even think of as my "conversations" with the Major.

However, my diplomatic reticence did not deter him from accelerating into full vitriolic stride once again upon his favourite subject of *bitter experience*, particularly as regarded his Hibernian charges: "You want my advice, Doctor, you'll keep a wary eye on the Irish. Give 'em any leeway, they'll…" I knew what was coming here and half-mouthed it silently as he did vociferously: *"…murder us in our beds."*

Another non-committal half-nod from me, as we reached the stable and heaved our saddles onto posts outside. Bascombe gave a silent sneer towards the interior, shook his head once more and turned back wordlessly towards the barracks.

I watched his lanky and lachrymose figure sliding mournfully away. Then I paused at the stable door, calling within: "Halloran?"

There was no answer. I called again, more forcefully: "Halloran, are you here?"

Shameless Halloran is not there, not at the stables - because at this moment he's hard at work in a paddock a short distance down the hill, out of sight and easy hearing of the barracks.

He pushes and pulls at the camel, yelling "SIT!" and "Get up there!" and other directions. All of them blithely ignored by "Carmel". She is having a very nice quiet time just where she is, and has far better things to do than be ordered about by another of these bellowing humans.

Jacky the native is standing by, looking faintly amused. After watching the Irishman struggle with the uncooperative dromedary for some time, the Aborigine at last strolls over and gently motions the sweating stablehand to stand aside.

Shameless is not too sure whether he should be doing what this grinning native suggests - but he consents to taking a few steps backwards and leaning in his familiar pose against a fencepost, waiting, a mildly suspicious look in his eye. What, he thinks, does this blackfellow think he can do with the beast that I cannot?

Jacky walks up slowly and fixes the camel with his eyes. They are sharply focused now, carrying not at all the vapid middle-distance stare he had worn earlier. He holds his hand up in a fist, index and little fingers raised in a horned shape. Tilting it to one side and then the other, still staring hard at the apparently mesmerised beast. "Koosh", he croons. "KOOOOSH."

Shameless finds himself once more open-mouthed - as Carmel closes her big eyes, sinks slowly to her knees and then topples gently over onto her side in a faint cloud of dust, apparently lulled into deep sleep.

Shameless stares at her prostrate form, then turns to Jacky.

"That's... that's amazin'!" And he turns back to gape down at the prone dromedary. As he does so, a quiet drawling voice replies most unexpectedly from close beside him:

"Little trick... picked up from Moorish trader."

Shameless shakes his head and turns sharply to Jacky, not quite believing his ears: "You what?"

The face looking back at the Irishman is not grinning stupidly now, as at their first meeting. Sharp and wry it is now, the eyes direct and twinkling. "All in wrist action," says Jacky.

Shameless blurts: "You... you can speak English!"

"A modicum," comes the modest reply. Then with a small grin: "Quite good with languages."

"But..." blurts the flabbergasted convict, "but why didn't you say so?"

Jacky considers this with a sardonic grin, thinking of his human company upon the recent expedition. "Little chance for... <u>intelligent</u> conversation, not lately." Rolls his eyes - but then nods in polite deference to the Irishman. "Until now, of course."

Shameless is wrong-footed anew by this backhanded flattery. "Well, I... thank you."

"Don't mention" comes the response. And then, conspiratorially, finger laid aside the broad dark nose: "Er, 'specially not to... Cap'n 'Great Explorer'. If you be so kind."

Jacky now snaps his fingers at the camel. She immediately begins to wake from her stupor and shake her great gangly limbs, sending up clouds of dust. The native hands the end of the bridle to the stablehand, and turns to saunter off up the hill.

Shameless is unable to keep the still astonished amusement out of his voice. "I'll, er... try to keep it under me hat!" he promises to the departing figure.

Then he shakes his head: Well, did you ever. He tugs on the bridle, crooning gently to the rising camel: "Come on, Carmel. Wakey wakey." And Carmel, now clambering to her feet, blinks her big, soft eyes and blinks languidly at him, as if to say "Oh dear, is it morning already?"

8. SADDLED

Not having found Halloran within, I had entered the stables and, after waiting a moment whilst my eyes adjusted to the gloom within, cast my gaze slowly around its interior.

At the far end was the stablehand's living quarter. This was plainly set up with a bed, table, small cupboard, and a very basic stone fireplace beneath a rudimentary chimney in the corner.

The remainder was the working area of the stables, which appeared an utter shambles to say the least.

Against the longer wall was a kind of small forge, with a furnace, anvil, hammers and various other tools for the working of metal. Along the walls to either side of this were a number of rough posts, racks and benches carrying an assortment of saddles, bridles, stirrups, girthstraps, spurs and other equestrian gear. Scattered about apparently at random - upon shelves, hooks and benches - were an assortment of tools; and hanging from the ceiling were a jumble of ropes, cords and chains suspended from an array of rude pulleys and wheels.

Brushing my way through the jungle of dangling ropes like some tropical explorer through a tangle of vines, I put my ill-fitting saddle down upon a bench and turned to the chaotic rows of gear - in search of a saddle whose dimensions might, in Bascombe's words, better match my arse.

As I moved along a row of saddles, my sleeve caught upon what appeared to be a small metal clasp. Unhooking myself from it, I found the clasp to be attached to the end of a fine ornate chain of some sort. The end of this chain disappeared behind a timber panel in the stable wall. I made a momentary effort to open this panel, but it was locked into place in some way and would not budge.

Curious to find such an object in the possession of a stablehand, I pondered this for a moment - and was sharply reminded of Bascombe's words: "Those that aren't thieves are robbers."

Unresolved as to what if any action to take about this discovery, I determined to do nothing at least for the moment and dropped the end of the chain, leaving it dangling where it was, as I turned back to the business at hand.

I moved again along the row of saddles, seeking a suitable one – so far without success. All were either too wide or were in obvious need of repair.

Finally, I turned to a pile of gear stacked in a corner – and found there, tucked away under a blanket, a quite presentable saddle, nicely worked about the edges. It appeared narrow enough, and though somewhat scratched, was apparently in sturdy condition. This, I determined, would clearly fit the bill, at least for the present.

I picked up the saddle and carried it outside. Placing it upon a post, I strode back to the barracks, untethered my mount, and led it to the stables where I raised the blanket over its back, and then reached for the new saddle.

At this point there was an approaching noise of slowly thudding hooves and an odd snorting noise - and around the corner of the building came the camel, led by Halloran.

What at first promised to be a grin of greeting from the stablehand turned quickly to something more like a grimace, as his eyes darted with a characteristic flash and he saw the activity upon which I was engaged.

"Here, what are you doin' with that?" he blurted - and then quickly added with belated respectfulness, "…er, sir?", as he quickly tethered the camel and scampered over to where I stood. I was surprised with what speed he could move for one so substantial.

"Well," I replied defensively, rather taken aback by his reaction and raising my voice slightly to achieve suitable authority, "I needed a narrower saddle than the one you'd given me. It was, I must say, extremely uncomfortable - and you not being here, I took the liberty of…"

He cut in quickly, words falling over each other, pupils in a frenzy. "No, well see, you can't take that one, doctor, it's… it's… not safe."

And then there was the slightest of pauses, but I fancied, a pause with some significance. A small glimmer came to his eye. It was as if he had in that instant sized me up, made some kind of assessment, and arrived at an instant decision to trust me with something rather important.

"Look," he said, "the girth is … broken."

With this he held up the said girth for my inspection. There was something oddly deliberate about his demeanour - the slightest suggestion, I half-fancied, of some ulterior motive. He appeared suddenly keen for me to examine the saddle closely. I resisted this for the moment.

"Where did you get this saddle?" I enquired, narrowing my eyes to peer closely at his face.

"I.. I never… I *found* it," he blurted out, unconvincingly.

"You *found* it? And where, might one ask?"

He drew a deep breath and answered, now quietly and with almost deathly calm: "On South Head beach, sir."

"On the *beach*? How did a fine saddle like this end up on the beach?"

He turned and looked at me very directly. "I found it there, sir. The day Dr Helfcott died. It belonged to him, sir."

He showed me the initials on the saddle: JFH. "Look there. Those are his initials. And look here." He showed me the broken girth strap, whose condition I admit I had altogether neglected to examine prior to making off with the saddle. I felt his eyes resting keenly upon me, waiting for my reaction after inspecting the state of the girth.

When I did so, my jaw dropped. "It's been… *cut* - almost right through," I gasped. And then with a sickening realisation: "My God. You know what this means…"

But now, just as suddenly, his tone had changed again, and eyes a-twinkle he chuckled teasingly: "Means you better not use it, sir. I'll get you another one." And with that he grabbed the saddle and darted off inside.

"Yes, but…" He having disappeared within, my only course was to quickly tether my horse and follow, as he rabbited on:

"Oh, don't worry sir, it'll fit you like a glove. Oh… and er, by the way, I'm pleased to tell you I've… managed to locate your trunk. It's inside."

This was good news indeed. "Ah!" A pause. "And its… contents?"

"All there, Your Doctorship… well, as far as I'm aware, sir." I nodded uncertainly at this.

Soon afterwards, the shadows lengthening outside, I sat within Halloran's stable, upon my trunk – which he had brought out proudly from beneath a pile of blankets, flinging them aside with a flourish as if performing a magic trick. All of its contents did indeed appear to be within, at least as far as I could tell upon cursory examination – though I could not be certain of the exact levels of the ingredients of all of the containers of tablets, spirits and other liquids.

A cosy fire was starting to flicker up from the rough stone fireplace near the stablehand's sleeping place. Lit by the pink glow spreading out from the flames, the suspicious saddle sat before us upon the table. I sat staring thoughtfully at it - as the Irishman, preferring perhaps due to his recent injury to shuffle stiffly around rather than join me upon the trunk, told me what he knew of the late Dr Helfcott.

"I'd got to know him quite well," he said. "A good man, Helfcott – kept himself to himself, as they say, but quite understandin' about a man's… little failin's. He'd give you the ointment without the sermon."

With this he winked, picked up a small bottle and filled a glass, offering it politely to me. Well, I thought, it couldn't hurt, not just the one.

"Er… thank you, Halloran, don't mind if I… er…" And as my glass was filled to the brim: "So who would have wanted to…"

"To do him in?" He shrugged. "I don't know, Doctor. He had no particular enemies, not that I'd heard of."

"And you'd hear of most things, I'd imagine."

"I try to keep me ear to the ground," he agreed modestly.

"Well then, could it have been… an affair of the heart, perhaps?" I prompted, warming to the melodramatic flavour of the issue. "Jealous lover?"

He shook his head fairly definitely. "The Doctor didn't go much for that sort of thing."

"Oh. Well then he… wasn't married? No family here?"

"Not a one. Quite a solitary man. Never spoke of family – never said anything at all about his life before comin' here."

I nodded, rolling the warming liquor around on my tongue. "Hmm, that is a very nice brandy, Halloran," I commented. "I rather fancy I have tasted a very similar one…"

This thought seemed vaguely to be leading somewhere, but Shameless seemed to have no desire to pursue a discussion of spirits and their respective qualities. He quickly stashed the bottle away out of sight and replied with an airy sweep of his hand: "Ah well, they er, they all taste the same, sir. After the first few." He appeared to wish to change the subject – perhaps, I thought, back onto the more interesting matter of the late Doctor.

"No, as I was sayin'," he continued, rubbing a leathery hand thoughtfully over his balding pate, "the one who cut the girth, would've had to be someone who was able to get at the saddle, in the first place… and who knew it was the doctor's…"

"Someone with access to Government House and the stables," I offered, starting to get into the swing of this.

"So not a convict then," he deduced.

"That's right." But then I glanced quickly sideways at him, possibly buoyed by the warmth of the liquor toward the liberty of a small mischievous prod: "Except of course that *you* would have enjoyed such access…"

He looked at me with a disapproving frown: "Now don't go thickenin' the plot unnecessarily, Doctor."

"Well, who, then?"

He shrugged. "I dare say we'll never know that, sir," he pronounced with almost dramatic finality. "Not now."

He turned away, narrowing his eyes just slightly. I may have been mistaken, but I rather fancied he knew that I would not let matters rest at this point - and I suspect, was even hoping that I would not.

"But look here," I objected, "we can't just leave it like that. Good God, man, there's… there's a *murderer* out there!"

He gave a twinkle, one shaggy eyebrow raised. "Possibly more than one, sir."

"No, I don't mean the convicts. We already ruled them out." But I could not resist adding once more, possibly just to keep him on his toes: "Except for *you.*"

"Don't go back there, Doctor", he cautioned again, impatiently.

"But look here…" I jumped restlessly to my feet now, bumping my head immediately on one of the rough low ceiling beams. Rubbing it, I tried again: "But look here, Halloran, there ought to be… an inquiry of some sort. Why haven't you told Major Bascombe about all this?"

He threw his head back and rolled his eyes. "This may come as something of a surprise to you, sir, but Major Bascombe is not in the habit of enterin' into detailed consultations with us convicts on matters of law and order. Especially not," he added, "with a feller who might be findin' himself a potentially prime suspect, as you've twice pointed out."

He slid his hand nervously beneath his shabby collar. "Breathe a word of it to him, an' I'd be findin' the term o' me natural life shortened by the approximate length of a stout piece o' hemp." And for good measure, "That's the way it is, sir."

"Just because it is," I countered, "doesn't mean it should be. Are you suggesting we should just… let it drop?"

"Well, better it than *me*," he determined, the hand at his neck sliding uncomfortably around under the collar.

"Hmm," I grunted. I could quite understand his reservation, but remained dissatisfied with taking no action at all about this most serious matter.

He looked at me, I fancied, just a little slyly - and then once again he lobbed in a deft and disarming change of subject: "Oh, by the way, sir, about tuning that piano…"

Now this was a subject I did not at all mind changing to, considering the attractive company into which it promised to lead me. "Ah yes," I responded keenly,"have you found anyone?"

"Well now… I think I've got just the man," he said with a smirk.

9. AN UNRESPONSIVE NOTE

I was not, it must be said, exactly what one might call a devotee of Irish music. From my observation of it, both before and especially since my arrival in the colony, it appeared to consist routinely of an unremarkable and indistinguishable series of inanely frenzied motifs throttled from badly tuned pipes, punctuated by thudding drum beats.

This was normally set to the visual accompaniment of a succession of Hibernian rustics capering absurdly on the spot, eyes fixed wildly upon an indeterminate point in the distance, arms pinioned like ramrods to their sides, while their legs flailed about in all directions at once in the manner of demented egg-whisks. Meanwhile their compatriots lurched about, clapping and whooping and, most significantly, drinking themselves rapidly into a stupor.

All in all, a most unedifying spectacle. Give me a nice quiet Mozart recital any day.

So it was a testament to the persuasive talents of Shameless Halloran upon the subject of his musical expertise that, in the face of my serious misgivings about the tonal sensibilities of the Irish, I had nevertheless acceded to being placed in my present position.

There I was, lying prone upon my back beneath the keyboard of the piano in the Strickleigh Ballroom at Government House – while Halloran, leaning upon the piano stool, issued instructions to me as to its tuning. The underside panel of the keyboard removed, I was engaged in the slow and painstaking business of tightening and loosening the pegs at the ends of the strings with a small jawed tool seconded from Halloran's stable, while he advised by how much each peg needed to be so adjusted.

"Now that one just there to the left… that's it, doctor, a quarter turn clockwise on that one, now."

I made the adjustment. He reached out one of those lazy digits and played the key. "That's better," he pronounced. I was relieved at this. In almost an hour, we had so far managed to tune a mere dozen of its several dozen strings.

In the background, dusting and polishing, was the maidservant Polly. She came bustling up behind him, peering over his shoulder for a moment, and eventually suggested: "There's a stool there. Wouldn't you be more comfortable sittin' down?"

"No I would not!" came the terse reply. Then he leant towards her and hissed with some irritation: "Wouldn't *you* be of more use *somewhere else?*"

"Well, pardon *me*," she said, some affront evident in her voice, and huffed out of the room.

The tuning continued for a few minutes more in relative silence, until Shameless said casually, as if making small-talk: "So, er… the Governor, then, he's a close relative of yours."

"Well," I replied after a moment's consideration, " 'close' is a 'relative' term. But in my family, 'relative' is not necessarily a 'close' one. Still," I added, "at least it brings Felicity within my ambit. My God, she's something, isn't she." I stopped work altogether at this point and unfocused my eyes to conjure up the glorious vision.

"She's certainly something, sir," he agreed pragmatically. "She's the daughter of the Governor. That is to say, your uncle," he added in pointed repetition.

The reference to my uncle somehow brought to my mind what I believed to be a rather clever idea. I sat up at once. "Look, I've been thinking. About the doctor's death… what if *I* were to raise it - with the Governor?"

Shameless appeared quite impressed with this, raising his bushy eyebrows: "Well now, that's a very good idea, Doctor. Don't know why *I* didn't think of it. His Excellency would have to take it serious, comin' as it would from his own nephew."

This, as it turned out, proved to be a most optimistic prediction of my uncle's response to my raising with him the the matter of Dr Helfcott and his untimely fall. A short time later I sat facing the Governor across his desk, the offending saddle upon it, as he threw back his head and half bellowed:

"Have you gone incurably *tropical?* That would have to be the most harebrained, preposterous notion I've ever heard. Where In Heaven's name did you get such a ridiculous idea?"

"I'm… not at liberty to say, sir," I mumbled. "Er, professional confidence, you know." I inwardly cursed the whole notion of raising the matter with the Governor – an idea, I was becoming increasingly certain, that had not really been mine at all, but had somehow originated with Halloran.

The Governor now stood up and came around his desk to stand over me, shaking his head in the utmost exasperation.

"Look here, Quayle, you can't go believing every potboiling yarn you hear from every second convict who comes staggering drunkenly through your surgery. Good God, man, if you had any idea of some of the…"

As he paused, presumably reaching for another contemptuous superlative, I jumped in quickly for a second attempt. "But Uncle…"

"I told you never to call me that!" he bellowed.

"Yes, quite so, er, Excellency, my apologies," I squeaked, took a quick breath and then attempted another foray: "But… sir, I believe there may be some substance in this," I persisted. "If there were an investigation…"

"There *was* an investigation!" he thundered. "It was conducted by Major Bascombe, who concluded after proper examination of all the relevant evidence that Dr Helfcott had fallen to his death quite by accident."

I could not help but leap to my feet. "But look, sir, the girth has been cut almost…" At this point I realised I was once again towering over my uncle, causing him to glare up at me in even greater annoyance. I hurriedly sat down again as he bellowed:

"But by whom, Quayle – and when? Before? After? In the water? On the beach? A month later? And how can we know when, where, why, or indeed by whom it was cut? Upon what reputable testimony?"

He glared at me. "Well?"

I had no answer to this, none that I could give him. I had a rather strong inkling that it would be a tad less than prudent to attempt to bring the word of a convicted forger to his unreceptive ears at this sensitive juncture.

My uncle remained standing, balancing upon the balls of his feet, and now pronounced with the unmistakeable tone he used when terminating a conversation:

"I think we've had quite enough of this nonsense." He brandished a stout finger at me. "Your career is already listing badly – don't sink it for good by allowing yourself to get carried away with flights of fancy from convict gossip-merchants whose own motives are *seldom if ever what they seem.*"

The state of my stomach at this point, already churning, was not greatly assisted by his reference to things listing and sinking. I merely gulped once and sat glumly, as he concluded ominously: "For the time being, at least, Quayle, you are a surgeon. I advise you very strongly to *do more of that.*"

10. THE BUSINESS OF THE COLONY

Soon afterwards I was "doing more of that", as my uncle had directed - though my mind remained at least partly fixed upon the Helfcott mystery.

At whose hand had this kind though reserved and enigmatic man met his demise, plummeting to his death from the South Head clifftop? What motive had prompted what person to tamper, deliberately and fatally, with the good doctor's girth-strap?

And more to the immediate point, how could I further the investigation of these mysteries without both incurring further displeasure from my uncle, and revealing the role of my convict colleague in my inquiries?

And there was one further, most perturbing question. If the doctor had met his fate because of something connected with his position here in the colony, was it not then possible that I, as his replacement in that position, might now also find myself facing danger on the same scale?

With these questions tumbling over each other in my mind, I ushered the last patient of the afternoon from my surgery, barely listening to her as she chirped away at me about goodness knows what ailment or symptom, whether real or imagined.

"Yes, Mrs O'Leary," I intoned politely. "Yes, yes, quite so. Well, you just let me know how that works, eh, and I'll have a look at it again next Tuesday. Yes, indeed so. Goodbye now."

I shut the door upon her and came back into the surgery. Taking advantage of a momentary lull in the flow of minor pestilence therein, I sauntered around behind my desk and sat down to think for a moment in the welcome silence.

Seeking to calm my nerves, I reached for a small flask and poured myself a half nip of brandy. Sipping it, I found to my displeasure that it did not taste nearly as good as I had expected it to - distinctly inferior, in fact, to that one of Halloran's. Was it going off in the heat, or were my taste buds being adversely affected by the climate, or perhaps by the stress of all this mystery? Ah, well.

After a minute - I am not certain whether it was more to catch up on some research, or to take my mind off the Helfcott mystery, or perhaps to gain some insight into the late doctor's work - for whatever reason, I rose and went to the bookshelf, taking down a dusty edition of "Gray's Anatomy" from the top shelf. This was one of a number of books left here by Helfcott.

I returned to my desk and opened the volume distractedly. It had clearly not been read for some time, a small cloud of dust ensuing from within as I flicked open the cover. From between the pages slipped several small sheets of paper that had been folded and inserted inside.

I examined these cursorily – mostly notes of a medical nature, page references for certain matters apparently arising from treatment of particular patients.

One loose page, however, was not of this nature – a single folded sheet of crumpled paper which I now spread out upon the desk. It was a wrinkled, worn legal-looking document, frayed about the edges, and carrying the faded heading "GRANT OF LAND".

I peered at it, frowning slightly. I beheld a name: PADRAIC MALARKEY; and other details of the grant of land to the said Malarkey, along with certain particulars of date and place - and at the base of the paper, the florid signature of "Sir Henry Blythe, Governor of His Majesty's Colony of Port Fortitude".

I pondered briefly upon this, wondering why such a document should have been here, slipped away within the pages of a textbook in the doctor's surgery. I concluded that it was most probably given to Helfcott by a patient for safekeeping.

After a moment, doubtful that it could be of any great significance, and hearing the knock of my next patient upon the door, I slipped the paper into a drawer and returned to my work.

On the hot dusty road around the outer perimeter of the Government House complex, a gang of convicts is working on the extension of the road towards the west – currently little more than a rough cart track once it reaches beyond the fringe of the clearing. The convicts, most of them wearing heavy leg chains, are overseen in their task by Captain Partridge and several armed troopers, shirts open under their red coats, leaning on their weapons in the sweltering heat while the Captain drawls the occasional cursory command.

These jail gangs provide the cheap labour for the construction of many roads, bridges and government buildings under Governor Blythe's ambitious program. They're already being contracted out to free settlers as farm labour. They'll provide a highly productive kick-start to the colony's economy – and to that of the fledgling nation.

Shameless Halloran and Jacky now come sauntering along towards this particular gang. A short distance from the work, they stop and observe.

"Still not comprehend," *says the native, rubbing his fingers through his dense curly hair,* "how being sent here is… punishment."

Shameless, whose mind is at this point rather occupied in pondering the mystery of the late doctor, answers him at first rather distractedly. "Well," *he mumbles,* "you know, it's the thing of bein' transported all this way… across the ocean, in chains…"

"But you said, these already prisoners, in rotting boats… unhealthy, getting sick…"

"Well yes, but at least it was home."

"And this is… not home?"

"Well, no. Not really. Not yet."

With this he returns to his deliberations upon the Helfcott matter, while Jacky thinks about this answer. These people have an oddly fixed idea, he thinks, about "home". He himself has employed this notion rather more flexibly, being used to a semi-nomadic life, moving about almost constantly from place to place within a defined tribal territory. What these people call home is something Jacky's mob would carry with them, from place to place. As the need arises. As the source of food dictates. Jacky is unaware at this point that in his own way, Shameless has also carried his home on his back.

"Better weather though", suggests Jacky now. "Bright sun, clean water, fresh food, better living. Much more... amenable, eh." He smiles, pleased with his appropriate use of this word.

The Irishman, his other train of thought now hopelessly shattered, considers this, scratching his head. "Well, yes. No doubt it is. When you look at it that way. Compared with where we've come from."

Jacky indicates the work gang: "And you say doing this... work here is... further punishment, on top of sending away from... home?"

"That's it," says Shameless, nodding.

The young native ponders this. "But how is work... punishment?" This is a novel concept, quite alien to the norms of his own society.

"Well," comes the almost defensive reply, "it is rather hot and hard work we do, all that farm clearin' and quarryin' heavy stone and all." The 'we', he knows, is a touch of poetic licence, since he himself has adroitly managed to avoid nearly all work of quite that level of strenuousness. He continues quickly: "And it's made a lot harder of late by the fact that our food rations seem to be gettin' smaller all the time, for some reason."

Jacky nods. "And these... law-breakers cannot refuse this... punishment, or be... <u>shunned</u> by your people?"

Shameless splutters slightly at this. "Well I think they'd get more than shunned, they'd cop a damn good <u>floggin'</u> for it."

"Ah yes," nods Jacky. "The... scarification ritual." He winces.

"That's the one."

"Very messy," opines the native, shaking his head with evident disapproval. And Shameless nods silently. Can't disagree with that.

Jacky frowns, puzzled, looks back at the workers. Notices the less impeded state of those more trusted. "But those without the chains, there, why they not... just run away?"

"What – into the bush? Ha!" Shameless guffaws. "Wouldn't last a week in there. Starve to death, for sure."

Jacky starts to grin. Ha, very amusing, eh. But then he realises the Irishman is not joking. In disbelief: "Starve? In this country? But food everywhere." He gestures expansively.

"Well, maybe to you, but they don't know how to find it, see, not like your *people do. In any case," scoffs the Irishman, "they'd never get far, not across the mountains. Quite impenetrable. Many a man's died tryin'."*

Jacky turns a canny eye to him. "That so? How you know this?"

"Well," the stablehand mumbles, "We've heard all the stories. From…" and he pauses, blinks at Jacky who is looking directly at him, and finishes quietly, beginning to realise where this is heading, "… from the er … the troopers."

"From troopers," repeats the native, nodding slowly. "Yes. But they not want any successful traverse of mountains… to become known, eh. To others. Might encourage… ideas of escape, eh."

"Well… yes, I suppose," admits Shameless slowly, "Yes, it might, at that. I can see what you're gettin' at, there."

And he ponders this for some moments. Jacky watches the gang at work. Again the native shakes his head. "Perplexing", he pronounces finally.

Then they walk on, the Irishman still frowning.

In the front garden bordering the commodious front lawn of the McMurdough farmhouse, another convict gang is at work: gardeners, planting busily from some of the pots unloaded earlier from the ship.

Lady Anastasia stands close by, dressed with her usual formality. She's supervising the convicts dictatorially, pointing with increasing exasperation.

"No no, the lantana goes <u>there</u>, the prickly pear <u>over there</u>, alongside the roses."

The men scramble to do her bidding. She continues imperiously, bombarding them with the sharpened stones of her instructions: "And mind you take care to water them every day. If these delicate specimens are to survive in this harsh landscape, they will require the utmost care."

Some of the plants in the McMurdough garden will indeed struggle in the hot, salty air of the mainland colonies. European flowers – primroses, wallflowers, rhodedendrons, roses – will battle here against the unfamiliar conditions, nurtured to reluctant maturity by obsessive gardeners hell-bent on floral colonisation. Meanwhile a great profusion of wildflowers thriving without human assistance in the nearby bushland will be scorned for many years as native and therefore inferior.

Some of the imported species will require no great maintenance. The lantana, bitou bush and prickly pear just planted at Anastasia's behest, along with the spiky gorse bush in the process of being busily imposed as a windbreak around the perimeter fences at the edge of the nearby pasture. These varieties are destined not only to survive but to thrive and prosper here - colonising vast areas and resisting all efforts to eradicate them or reduce their rapacious spread.

Such efforts at control will include the introduction of a variety of creatures which are intended to devour these noxious plants. Not only will none of these creatures prove equal to the task - or in many cases, even much interested in it - but most will go on in turn to be classified as significant pests in their own right. This will prompt a new generation of extermination experts to devise newer, bigger and more grotesque methods of wiping out these creatures - again routinely with minimal success and to the detriment of land and life. Nevertheless these experiments will continue, undaunted and undeterred by their demonstrable failure. Such is to be the biological destiny of this continent.

But the Great Lady of McMurdough Farm knows nothing of this. She is concerned only with asserting her dominance over her immediate environment. She grits her teeth. She is determined to impose, maintain and defend her small and ordered piece of European culture, transplanted so forcibly into this savage landscape. That is what colonising is about, after all: one must move in and establish control. Firmly and without compromise.

With a final glare at the foreman she turns on her heel and marches haughtily off up the path towards the house.

The gardeners turn and look at each other, rolling their eyes. This will be a long, hard assignment. They have faced hard labour on many occasions and under many masters, but this lady must surely be the worst slave-driver in the Empire.

11. HALLORAN HISTORY

From my conversations with Shameless, together with the diverse accounts of other convicts and some of the officers, particularly the accommodating Captain Partridge, I was able to piece together something of the Irishman's life story up to this point.

His earlier years were clouded in some degree of mystery. Accounts of them differed widely – even his own, which appeared to ebb and flow upon mutable waves of necessity, convenience and self-justification.

This much, however, was clear: Seamus Halloran had grown up in the hard back streets of Dublin, and had developed from quite an early age a keen eye for either small business, or crime - depending on one's point of view.

As a youth he had drifted naturally into a scrabbling existence among the "cornerboys", the gangs of youths loitering about street corners earning a crust by whatever means they might, legal or otherwise. Somehow the image of him leaning against a lamp-post on a Dublin corner conformed most obligingly with my first sight of him, propped against the navigation post on the beach, his mind as always upon his next profitable transaction. He was smart, no doubt of it, and had managed despite his meagre origins to learn to read and write after a fashion, and to tally up figures – the latter skill soon put to good use.

Upon Dublin's mean streets he had undoubtedly played a pivotal role in a goodly range of transactions, presumably upon both sides of the law.

He had also, it seemed, spent some time moving about the countryside with the "travelling people", the home-grown Irish gypsies; and it was with them that he had developed his affinity with horses, learning to train and handle them – and presumably, how to remove them without a whinny, and without a word of permission, from the premises of their rightful owners.

There were also stories alluding to his extraction of income from a variety of other sources – including the manufacture of "poteen", the local illicit liquor, and its distribution in Dublin's "shebeens" or sly grog shops.

He was born, by his own admission, with the "gift of the gab"; and it was said by some that the young Mr Halloran had applied this talent to a spot of "bludging" – business-minded partnership with certain ladies of the night, from whom he could derive a modest commission for his undoubtedly skilful promotional efforts.

He himself would admit only to "actin' as an agent for certain ladies in the entertainment profession" and raised his eyebrows with self-righteous indignation at the suggestion that he would allow himself to be connected with behaviour of an immoral kind. "Sure an' that kind o' thing'd be against me religion," he protested.

There was no suggestion from any quarter of his having ever been involved in wrongdoing of a violent nature – though whether this scruple arose from principled motives or was simply based on his pragmatic avoidance of danger… well again, this depended upon one's viewpoint of the man and his motives.

In any case, he managed to elude the clutches of the law until around the turn of the century, when he was arrested in the harsh crackdown following the Irish Rebellion of 1798. This uprising was inspired at least in part by the American and French revolutions which preceded it. If the French had thrown off their autocratic rulers (even if, as it turned out, they had then proceeded to replace them with equally autocratic ones), well then, reasoned the Irish, why could they not do likewise? And if America could win its independence from the hated British and forge a republic, then why not Ireland?

Shameless was always quick to associate his own arrest with the nationalistic ideals of the '98 uprising, casting himself in ringing tones as an honest and patriotic victim of brutal repression.

The officers were scornful of this, pointing out that his crime was not, after all, sedition or anything of the kind, but forgery.

"I'm afraid our Mr Halloran's arrest had little to do with politics," Partridge laughed, "and rather more to do with pockets – his own, and the lining thereof."

Indeed, observed the affable Captain, when Halloran spoke of his "nationalistic spirits" he was most probably alluding to the poteen he'd sold with characteristic opportunism to young insurgents in need of a little something to fire up their rebellious zeal. He'd been quick to profit, chuckled Partridge, from the climate of insurrection; and, the babyfaced Captain asserted, it had been in furtherance of his poteen trade that Halloran had sought to augment his capital with an injection of artificially produced currency. He had simply grown too cocky, too big for his boots – or, Partridge added with a hoot, "too fat for his breeches, rather" - and had suffered the consequences.

Whatever the truth of all this, Shameless Halloran had found himself suddenly imprisoned, carted off to a jail in the English midlands, and finally sent to Portsmouth to be shipped away to the colonies.

Upon the voyage out he had quickly become something of an organising point for the convicts, a go-between pleading with the authorities on their collective behalf and conveying information to them.

It was reputed that he also organised illicit wagering events staged in the darkened bowels of the ship, involving the staking of food and drink rations upon the competing progress of captured cockroaches along the creaking floor of the cramped convict berths (my stomach turned anew at the mere thought of those conditions – and the memory of my own journey). It was believed that his own rations had been considerably augmented by his success in the staging of these events. Certainly he had reached the colony no thinner than before – unlike so many others.

He had arrived in Port Fortitude seven years hence, and had kept his head down for some five years afterwards - sufficiently to gain his ticket-of-leave status.

He had then basically talked his way into the post of colonial stablehand upon the release of its previous occupant, by demonstrating his knowledge of horses and stables. He adroitly neglected, of course, to raise the potentially awkward question of whether he had had any legitimate business being within the stables in which he had gained such experience. In the absence of any other suitable candidate (an absence quite possibly secured by various forms of bribery of other contenders to stand aside in his favour), he was given the stablehand's position. This he had by all accounts filled with a fair degree of competence, only the irascible Bascombe voicing any substantial reservations upon this issue.

Shameless was generally well regarded by his fellow convicts, as a man whose heart was – "generally", "in the circumstances", "as much as could be expected", and so on - in the right place.

Even the officers, with the predictable exception of the Major, had a variety of grudging regard for him. Partridge confessed to really quite liking the fellow, and said the officers often found him valuable as a kind of informal conduit to the convict mood. He was never quite an informer, more a useful middleman between the troopers and their arrowhead-tailored charges. Shameless could be relied upon to let the officers know what was likely to be the convict response to various tasks and measures, to offer constructive suggestions, and in general to act in a way that somehow tended to keep things calm in that quarter. While Bascombe ranted about him stirring up trouble, the reality was that his presence in any crisis tended, on the whole, to achieve the reverse.

He was routinely suspected by the officers – and would have been willingly hung without trial by the Major, and indeed drawn and quartered for good measure - for every disappearance of every saleable item in the colony. Such disappearances were certainly not infrequent. However, despite all of Bascombe's best endeavours, neither he nor any other officer had ever managed to gather sufficient evidence to sheet home any such theft to the beaming Irishman.

Yes, he was smart, and no two ways about it. His "years of undetected crime", if indeed they were, appeared set to continue for some time yet.

He had never married. Had there been women in his life? Most assuredly – indeed, on the one occasion when I had asked him this question he had beamed broadly and responded with a wink: "Oh, *hundreds*, sir, *hundreds.*"

Well, certainly there had been several, according to other sources. The most recent, reportedly, involved a fellow convict employed in the Government House kitchens, though I could find no reliable confirmation of this. No one female figure, it seemed, had loomed particularly large in his life – or "not since me dear old mother", he asserted with theatrical reverence.

In our single discussion of such affairs of the heart, he at first chuckled that "No woman could ever keep up with me"; then he frowned and shrugged and spoke of a definite reluctance to maintain a romantic liaison for any length of time.

"Yer go down that path too far an' they start makin' demands – and' then where are yer? Things start getting' complicated. A man's gotta have his… little secrets."

Then he had touched his finger aside of his nose and, in his characteristic fashion, the subject was deftly changed with a grin and a darting of the pupils, any small shiny treasures of that kind locked safely away behind the secret panels of Halloran's heart.

12. A GRAND OCCASION

In his quarters, the meticulous self-sprucing of Captain Ffeffington-Weekes in preparation for the Great Banquet has gone well. Thanks (though no thanks are given) to the forced assistance of a small army of convict servants, all of whom have been treated with the Captain's usual lofty contempt.

The Great Explorer is now well and truly trimmed, brushed, powdered. Smartly uniformed, sashes and braids in gaudy array, brass buttons and buckles at full shine. He stands before his mirror, painstakingly pruning the tips of his ginger moustache to pointed perfection. He seems very pleased indeed with the ensuing vision smirking back at him from the glass.

Yes, a most fitting personage, concludes the Captain, to stand before the Royal Society. The Great Banquet, to him, will be little more than a dress rehearsal for that inevitable bravura performance, the crowning glory of his heroic exploits.

His eyes water and he licks his lips hungrily at the very prospect.

Most assuredly not licking his lips at this same moment is Geoffrey Bascomb. Rather, his long face twitches and sneers and bucks at its sidelevers with some irritation at the Governor's unwillingness yet again to acknowledge that his, the Major's, view of things is the only sensible one. In this case, his view of the stuffed-shirt Great Explorer and his planned Big Event.

"Well, if I may say, sir," huffs the Adjutant, as Blythe signs more papers with a weary and cursory glance, "it does seem a great deal of effort in honour of a rather ill-prepared adventure, with little evidence of any actual…"

The Governor cuts him off firmly, advances on his subaltern from behind his desk. Oh dear, thinks the Major, lucky me, here comes another of his bloody tirades.

"That 'adventure' as you call it, Bascombe," huffs the Governor, "will almost certainly result in Captain Ffeffington-Weekes being admitted to the Royal Society, a body brim-full of the most respected scientific minds in the length and breadth of the Empire. Can you muster any appreciation of the value of the positive publicity that such an address could bring to Port Fortitude?"

Blythe well understands the imperative - and the considerable difficulty - of attracting free settlers across the ocean to this far-flung outpost. He's already begun the daunting task of inducing them to leave their safe Britannic niches and relocate to Port Fortitude. Commissioned at some cost the writing and despatch to England of florid accounts of the colony's lush farmlands, hospitable climate, grand commercial prospects. Even gone so far as to engage an artist to paint appealing pictures of the settlement to be sent back to the Mother Country.

This artist was a botanist renowned for his skill in the meticulous drawing and painting of landscapes and flora. In fact, rather too meticulous, thought the Governor - the fellow's first attempts far too drily accurate, conveying altogether too much of the strange and daunting harshness of this wide brown land. One might as well be inviting people to the moon, scoffed Blythe. The painter was duly commanded in no uncertain terms to forego such gritty realism and instead to marshal his artistic talents toward making Port Fortitude's pastures and gardens appear a good deal greener, gentler, more symmetrical, more ordered and... well, more <u>English</u>.

The botanist had huffed and whinged and finally agreed with great reluctance to amend his master works. But upon one condition: that he would be honoured for his efforts – perhaps, he'd suggested, by having a species of plant named after him.

The Governor had slyly agreed. Certainly, Mr Patterson, he had promised, it will be done. You have my solemn word.

And from that time onward a pestilent purple plant pervading farmlands across the continent would be known as "Patterson's Curse".

Some of the botanist's artworks will also survive, however. In future years, *art historians will look back patronisingly on these early colonial daubings as examples of how painters struggled to depart from their European visual standpoint and to accurately interpret the radically different shapes and textures of the Australian landscape – its pale, bright-edged light quality, its unusual curling plant forms, and so on. Without being there, how could these critics have known how little such lack of accuracy owed to cultural standpoint or visual misperception, and how much it arose instead from obeisance to the stern dictates of economic imperative.*

This remains the Governor's singular priority. He finds it exasperating that his subordinates, including Bascombe, fail to grasp the importance of it. He finishes his tirade and crosses his arms upon his chest, scowling at his Adjutant.

The latter's sideburns now bristle with indignation and his prominent chin starts to quiver defensively. "Yes, of course, I understand all that, Excellency," *he mumbles grudgingly and unconvincingly,* "but really, putting on banquets and what-have-you, when…"

Again Blythe cuts him off, choosing to end the exchange at this point rather than quibble any further with this annoying lack of vision. "Appearances are important, Bascombe. We must attract the better class of free settler to the colony. And to do that, we must portray it as a place of…" *(the final words emphasised in habitual fashion)* "<u>steady progress and quiet efficiency.</u>"

Steady progress and quiet efficiency would not appear to be greatly in evidence in the Government House kitchens at early evening. That dubious sanctum is a noisy hullabaloo of crashes, clashes and clangs. Shouting and shoving. Cooks and servants dashing in all directions.

In the midst of it stands Polly, hands on hips, looking even pinker than usual in the heat and smoke and steam, as around her careers the chaotic preparation of large quantities of food. The roasted carcasses of several fat pigs lie steaming upon the table, being busily garnished with vegetables. Well, thinks Polly, at least we got this lot before they scarpered into the bush.

The maidservant has been placed in charge of the movement of all the food from the kitchens to the banquet hall. As she shouts orders through the mayhem, she is almost beheaded by someone reaching up to hang an implement on a hook overhead. "Owww, bloody 'ell, Mavis, mind what you're doin' with that bleedin' ladle," shrieks Polly. "You damn near brained me!"

Mavis, the plumpish head cook, merely smiles unabashedly and turns to give a leisurely stir to an enormous tank of soup bubbling on the stove behind her.

Polly's keen eye now catches another movement and perceives a presence she's been waiting impatiently for. The face and frame barreling into the kitchen is unmistakeable even in the ill-fitting waiter's outfit. He and many other convicts have been hastily dragooned into assisting with this enormous social endeavour. Polly notices his darting eyes in their usual manner hastily taking in the details of the kitchen, a chamber most certainly not within his normal ambit of operations.

She turns to him and hands him an enormous stack of crockery. " 'Ere, Shameless – get the rest of those dishes up on the table quick smart. The guests are arrivin'."

Someone else has also noticed the Irishman's presence: Mavis the cook catches his eye for the briefest of moments before averting it towards the soup. Is there a slight wink from him and a momentary blush upon her cheek? Or is this no more than our imagination at play, his eye blinking only because of the steam and her cheek merely reddened by the heat of the kitchen?

In any event, by the time she looks up again he has staggered off with a grunt of exertion, the pile of plates rattling and tottering precariously.

At the front entrance of Government House, the guests are beginning to arrive in a procession of transplanted European finery. All are keenly aware that here, perhaps even more than back in England, one's position in society is manifest in one's manner of dress. Every effort has been made by the guests to marshal their finest attire – a task rendered more difficult by the scarcity in the colony of fine cloth and of skilled tradespeople to weave, sew, embroider or otherwise embellish it.

The guests are met at the front door in a flourish of formal greeting by Governor Blythe, his daughter and the Adjutant. The Governor and the Major sport full military sashes and braids, hats held formally in cocked elbows; Felicity is resplendent in a spectacular bright blue ballgown, her hair piled in high cascades.

Bascombe exhibits his customary air of stiff, dutiful tolerance. Nods with wordless formality at each guest in turn. Sir Henry, however, despite his earlier impatience with his daughter on the subject of social imperatives, is now quite enjoying himself in the grandeur of the occasion.

"Ah, Dr Mountfort, good evening to you... and to you, Mrs Mountfort", booms Blythe to the colony's rather amply proportioned private doctor and his wife.

"Governor... Miss Felicity..." *Mountfort beams, removes from his mouth a large carved Meerschaum pipe. Exhales a pungent cloud of black smoke over the welcoming party. They accept this without any thought of protest, though with some inadvertent coughs and splutters. Oblivious, the doctor reaches out to shake the Governor's hand and then bends to kiss Felicity's. He looks up to acknowledge Bascombe with a minimal* "Major"*, before propelling his wife towards a group of conversing ladies and, dusting his hands with the air of one who has succeeded of getting rid of an encumbrance, waddling off in search of a decent game of cards – a passion for which he's well known.*

More guests appear: first, a group of military officers, scrubbed up and shining. Most, like Partridge, apparently single; a smaller number with young wives, giggling with nervous excitement, clutching onto their soldiers' arms.

Now a group of settlers, including the botanist, Patterson – tall and angular, scowling slightly at the Governor, still smarting, it seems, over his less than favourable immortalisation as a floral curse.

And now the McMurdoughs sweep in. She in elegant cream satin, he in uniform now - and as starched, stiff and stolid as ever. He removes his semicircular Napoleonic hat to reveal the carefully brushed dark thatch beneath, its unmentionably French curl fully in evidence thanks to Anastasia's attention to it.

At his superior's arrival, Bascombe quickly and with evident relief hands over the greeting duties to McMurdough, excuses himself, and slips quickly away with a darting, purposeful glance.

The Governor, meanwhile, returns the Colonel's salute with a polite though unenthusiastic "McMurdough. Good to see you."

"Excellency," *nods the military commander.* "Yes, I was, er... wanting to talk to you about the new strain of short-horned sheep I have imported from Spain. Magnificent specimen – a reputation for great virility, and yet up to this point does not seem to be able to...."

Sensing that this turn of conversation may not be suitable for female ears – nor, when it comes to that, for anybody's - the Governor cuts him short as one would a small child: "Yes yes, later, McMurdough, tell me about it later." *And turns smoothly to the Colonel's wife:* "Lady Anastasia. If I may say, you are looking quite splendid tonight."

Anastasia bows slightly, lowering her eyes with long-practised demureness. Felicity sees an opportunity and steps forward, scanning the lady with ill-disguised disdain. Talk about mutton dressed as ham.

She chirps in with an edge: "Yes, I've… <u>always</u> admired that dress… " *and she adds in pointed avoidance of the courtesy title of "Lady" to which her addressee has been accustomed:* "… <u>Mrs</u> McMurdough."

Anastasia turns towards the young upstart sharply. If looks could kill, hers would personally inter the corpse, deliver the funeral oration and send out the Thank You notes for every condolence letter. She counters with a lofty sneer at the precocious minx's rather luridly hued gown: "And I've always admired your… <u>courage</u>, my dear."

Felicity with great difficulty forces a smile, her eyes looking not merely daggers but a whole arsenal of finely-honed implements at her keenly perceived social competitor. She is visibly coiling for a rejoinder when her father wisely intervenes: "Yes well, Felicity, I think you should move to the piano now, it's almost time for your recital…"

His daughter opens her mouth slightly but closes it again. Forces another grim smile, and slithers away towards the Strickleigh Ballroom. The Governor exhales with relief at the defusing of the escalating hostilities.

"If you would excuse me for just a moment," *says Anastasia, with a slight sneer towards the young woman's departing form,* "I think I need some… fresh air before dining. I shall join you shortly."

The others move aside for her. Colonel McMurdough shrugs vaguely as his wife sweeps off along the corridor and around the corner, out of their view.

Her features now tinged with a strange urgency, she turns quickly to check that she is not being observed, and slips noiselessly out through a side door.

As she glides away from the building towards the stables, a face appears cautiously from behind the wall. A sharp, worry-worn face, framed by twin columns of bristle which almost stand on end as he waits tensely in the darkness.

As Geoffrey Bascombe sees Anastasia approaching, his eyes flash with a spark not of anger or bitterness but of something else. Something wild and distant. Something never seen in public, framed between those hirsute brackets.

Now the grand lady sees him. A faint smile crosses her lips, muscles in her thin cheeks twitching.

They move towards each other in the shade of the wall... and there they embrace passionately in a near-electric rustle of starched fabric, a small but audible moan escaping from the Major and almost a gasp from the lady at the ferocity of his caress.

But almost immediately, this secretive and illicit dalliance is interrupted by the sound of a horse neighing close by. Bascombe glances about nervously. Anastasia grips his arm firmly and draws him quickly behind the wall, out of sight. There they wait in nervous and impassioned breathlessness.

Slowly, a figure emerges from the darkness. No, not one but several figures. The first of them is Jacky, and the remainder are several guests' horses which he is leading from the Government House forecourt towards the stables. Their nostrils puff steam into the night air, hooves thudding into the grass.

The native saunters by, not turning his head, appearing quite unaware of the close proximity of scandal lurking furtively in the shadows.

I could not help but be impressed by Felicity's pianoforte recital. To be honest, I was at this point oblivious to any musical flaws my young relative may or may not have possessed, being as I was, concerned more with examining her delightful features as she struggled gamely with the music. I must admit, however, that I did notice some other people, including Polly who was working quietly nearby, wincing at perhaps the odd imperfectly-played note.

I had, there was no mistaking, become rather infatuated with my gorgeous cousin. Back home in England, my attempts at courtship had never really gone as planned – somehow I had never quite been able to follow the initial halting approaches with sufficient determination, the relationships left dangling messily like one of my uncompleted surgical operations. In the back of my mind lurked the dim hope that somehow, here in the colonies, a fresh start might be made and I might fare better in this regard, as well as in my professional duties.

As the recital concluded, I broke into enthusiastic applause, which I restrained slightly at the realisation that the response of the rest of the audience was somewhat less fulsome.

As the others shuffled rather quickly away, I stepped forward to congratulate my cousin: "Very good, Lady Felicity. Well played."

The grin fell from my face as she at once turned to snap at me: "Hm. No thanks to your tuning. The nearest that piano came to a musical note was the squeak of the stool as I sat upon it. If your handling of medical instruments matches your handling of musical ones, the undertaker will soon be working double shifts."

I stood rooted to the spot, mouth open, blinking with shock, struck dumb - and more so when she immediately turned from me, her scowl transformed to a beaming smile as she greeted: "Ah, Captain Ffeffington-Weekes!"

She moved to the explorer, he much transformed from when I had last seen him with the camel. He was now glittering with military braid, moustache waxed to sparkling pinpoints. He stepped forward to meet her, taking her hand and kissing it elegantly. She fluttered her eyelashes at him, he not favouring me with so much as a glance of acknowledgment before sweeping her off upon his arm.

I could do nothing but move sadly away. As I did so, I numbly observed Shameless shuffling about clearing away plates of *hors d'oeuvres*. As he did so, he appeared to be examining items upon the tables with very keen interest.

I looked towards Felicity again and found her hanging upon the damned explorer's every word.

Seeking perhaps some solace in conversation, I turned back to where Shameless had stood; but he was gone. I looked around but could not see him anywhere.

Dinner proceeded dreadfully slowly - culminating in an interminable speech by Ffeffington-Weekes upon his epic adventures on the Great

Expedition. He outlined in excruciating detail, illustrated by elaborate maps, the exact route of his journey; he expostulated at length upon the landforms and the flora and fauna he had discovered; and he described in vivid and no doubt creative detail the great dangers and terrible depredations he had endured, and the extraordinary bravery he had exhibited in overcoming them.

"… and sixthly," he intoned as I reached once more for the brandy bottle, "I can definitely announce that the Great Inland Sea has not only been found… but *circumnavigated!*"

He beamed, blue eyes shining with something approaching hysteria as he soaked up the applause from his captive audience. Felicity, of course, was his most attentive listener, applauding most enthusiastically of all.

13. NOT-SO-GREAT EXPLORATIONS

Shameless Halloran has awaited his chance to slip unnoticed from the ballroom. The sleeves of his waiter's jacket jangle softly with secreted silverware as he scuttles across the Government House courtyard and heads for the stables.

Arriving there, he's found Jacky in one of the stalls, scraping away with a shoeing hammer at the hoof of a guest's horse. After a brief but jovial greeting to the native, Shameless has moved to the far wall. Now, with his back to Jacky, his actions masked by his own ample frame, he sets about examining the purloined items with a well-trained eye – slipping each one soundlessly into a shelf concealed behind one of his many hidden panels in the wall.

Jacky, apparently quite oblivious to this, does not look up from his work as Shameless, over his shoulder, engages him in conversation as to what has really happened on the Great Expedition. Slowly the true story unfolds.

"...So now we come back to same place for... fifth time," says the native, "after going several hundred miles, 'as crow circles'..."

Shameless chuckles.

"Finally, using er, 'primitive sign language', I convey to him, perhaps *I* should drive for a bit. Take him to nice lake – he rushes up, screaming 'Great Inland Sea, Great Inland Sea!' And... falls right in! Sploosh!"

"Ha! What a buffoon!" the stablehand guffaws, imagining the slapstick scene; while his hands, hidden behind his ample torso, quietly slip another engraved fork into its cache behind the secret panel.

"Meanwhile I," continues Jacky, "make big show of 'negotiating with savages', and get some social calls in. Lot of family up that way. Cousin's people, mostly. Funny," he thinks aloud, "Great Explorer wants to 'boldly go where no man has ever gone before'; for me it's... a chance to drop in on the relatives."

A point well made. Shameless nods and grins. Another fine silver spoon slides away safely out of sight.

"Anyway," Jacky continues, "stayed there for a bit, catching fish – well, *I* caught, he ate - until he was strong enough for 'heroic return'."

Shameless half turns, hands momentarily empty. "So how long did it take youse to come back?"

"Oh, same time as getting there," *Jacky winks confidentially.* "Paid by the day."

Shameless grins. A beat, the crickets chirping. He purses his lips pensively. "I was thinkin' – we don't see many of your people around here. Hardly any, come to that."

Jacky sits up slightly, eyes still upon his work. "No, well – we have saying: 'Location, location, location'. This place, bad location. Swampy, sandy, too many mosquitoes – altogether, best avoided." *He shakes his head.* "Don't get why your mob chose right here to set up camp – poorest position on whole coastline."

Shameless chuckles. "Don't think we actually had much choice in the matter. As I understand it, the ship's captain was a drunkard, vessel went miles off course, ripped its hull out on a reef, ran aground on the north headland an' sank like a stone. Straight to the bottom. Captain was dead drunk, fast asleep below. Went down with the ship. The crew were surprised the volume of alcohol he'd consumed, bein' lighter than water, wasn't sufficient to raise him immediately to the surface, and the whole ship with him." *Jacky shakes his head with amusement.*

"So that was how Port Fortitude was founded," *Shameless concludes.* "Of course, that wasn't its original name – the crew at first gave it a much less printable title – an' I'm not at all sure they weren't right."

Jacky smiles again. Shameless cocks his head and asks him: "So… why does yourself stay here?"

The native shrugs. "Thought I might… pick up useful skills, new tools… you know, to take back to family."

"And have you found any?"

"Not a lot." *He thinks.* "That camel could be useful. Good on sand."

Shameless grins, turning back to his stash. "By the way, do you have a real name?"

"Of course," says Jacky, and he pronounces it. There is a pause.
"Not an easy one to, er, get yer tongue around," says Shameless, embarrassed.
"Languages not your strong suit, you people. Well, 'Jacky' do for now, eh?" smiles the native forgivingly, and bends down again to work on the horseshoe. As he does so he adds, in the same leisurely drawl, and still without looking up:
"By the way, nice silverware. Should get good price for that."
Shameless almost jumps out of his skin, spinning around, bumping the panel with a loud crash of silver, one or two pieces dropping to the floor in front of him. Guilty as sin, mouth gaping once again, he croaks: "You what?"
Jacky grins and winks at him, reassuringly. And Shameless rather awkwardly returns the grin, reassured that his secret is quite safe in these steady, dark hands.

The mighty aquatic body so earnestly sought by the Great Explorer – and so comically 'discovered' by him - will occupy the attentions of a good many more deluded adventurers. All are obsessed with tracking the destinations of the several rivers discovered heading inland, which they find to their surprise flow not eastwards towards the sea, but to the west – towards.... what?

Many explorers, both before and after Ffeffington-Weekes, are convinced that these rivers must flow into a vast sea in the centre of the continent. A succession of far-fetched, speculative maps will be duly drawn up and a procession of fervent and elaborately-equipped expeditions despatched in search of the great reservoir. All will return in feverish defeat, with presumably sun-addled tales of rivers disappearing into thin air.

And some of these explorers will never return, wandering bravely but suicidally off into the desert in search of the mysterious waterways, to perish from lack of water and/or food - while the bemused indigines look on, scratching their heads, unable to comprehend how these pale visitors can so comprehensively fail to utilise the plentiful resources of their environment.

No Inland Sea will ever be discovered – because, of course, it doesn't exist. The rivers, perhaps wisely escaping the heat, simply disappear underground into subterranean watercourses that bubble langorously upwards some distance later to join and thread their leisurely way southwards through the semi-arid landscape towards their ultimate destination: the Great Australian Bight and the Southern Ocean.

The Inland Sea, like so many dreams in the Great South Land, will prove to be no more than a trick of the light.

But Captain Ffeffington-Weekes is oblivious to all this – as, fair to say, to most things beyond the vast expanse of his own ego. As the evening wears on inside the banquet hall, he continues to sound off on his "discovery" of the mythical reservoir, among his other exploits - his exposition seemingly as limitless as his vanity. The audience has by now lost all traces of enthusiasm and is sinking rapidly into a stupor, lulled by the explorer's soporific tones. Even Felicity is now unable to suppress a small yawn, though expertly concealed behind her gloved hand.

Polly moves around busily. She's forced to cover progressively greater distance due to the diplomatic necessity of giving a wider and wider berth to the Reverend Staines. Specifically, to avoid the increasingly drunken wanderings of his wine-tainted hands.

At last the Great Explorer, in front of an array of Aboriginal spears and implements, appears to be droning toward what sounds – to those still awake – promisingly like a conclusion:

"… heralds a new era of expansion and development for our great colony. And so ladies and gentlemen, I give you… Port Fortitude!"

His audience, relieved, raise their glasses and drink. Felicity gazes at the Captain adoringly.

Dinner had been dispensed with – rather sooner than I had expected, by virtue of finding that for some reason I had not been given a dessert-spoon. Nevertheless I was quite ready to forego additional nourishment in the interest of being spared further servings of the intolerable public posturing of Ffeffington-Weekes. I had escaped to the drawing room, where I was now ensconced in a comfortable if somewhat lumpy armchair.

I looked slowly about the room.

At a table in one corner was Dr Mountfort, with whom I had been singularly unsuccessful in striking up a professional conversation – he apparently regarding a colonial surgeon, ministering to mere convicts, as being so far inferior to him in the medical and social pecking order as to be beneath contempt.

I had first been introduced to the good doctor by Major Bascombe, soon after my arrival. On that occasion we had arrived at the doctor's comfortable cottage to find him apparently in the midst of hosting a luncheon for a small handful of well-to-do free settlers. Upon Bascombe's brusque formal introduction at the door, Mountfort had given a half-snort, half-chuckle and scornfully opined that mine was a fruitless task, since in his view convicts were as a rule quite incapable of taking even the most minimal steps to control their self-indulgent vices to the extent necessary to maintain themselves in good health. Then he had given me a brief handshake, wished me well and virtually slammed the door in our faces.

This evening, when I had made another attempt at medically-based conversation, he had merely repeated, loudly and for the benefit of all present, his pessimistic pronouncement upon convicts and their incorrigible unhealthiness – exhaling as he did so an enormous cloud of acrid pipe-smoke upon me. This, as with so many strong odours, elicited from my sensitive stomach such a wave of nausea that I was quite unable to respond.

It occurred to me that perhaps word had also reached Mountfort, upon the well-nourished colonial grapevine, of my previous inglorious professional history. In any case, he had made no secret of his determination to exclude me both from the subsequent conversation and from the ensuing game of cards. He now sat smoking and smirking, a pile of coins before him upon the baize-topped table as he dealt another hand to a murmuring cabal of well-heeled settlers and officers – among whom I noticed Captain Partridge laughing and drinking and puffing along.

A little distance away, I was dimly aware of a conversation within a standing group comprising the Governor, the McMurdoughs and the Reverend Staines. At the edge of this group, lurking in limbo between them and me, was Major Bascombe.

My uncle was in full voice, holding court. "But you see, the whole *point* of our rehabilitation policy is that it allows the colony to benefit from the labour of convicts, while they in turn benefit from being put to an honest day's work."

Colonel McMurdough appeared less than convinced by this, drawling: "Lucky if you can get an honest *hour* out of them."

"That is certainly true of some," responded the Governor calmly, "yet some work well enough – and many have been prepared to grasp the second chance in life afforded to them, and have gone on to pay their debt and become productive members of our society."

At this, Anastasia interpolated tartly: "That may be just as well, since free settlers are not exactly swarming here like bees to nectar." And she added quickly, aside to her husband, as if to head off any confused interjection from that quarter: "A *simile*, Montague."

The Governor replied steadily: "They will come, Lady Anastasia, they will come." And he added with a grim half-smile: "We must be patient."

At this came the slurred voice of the Reverend, blurting out: "Aye, the patience of Job. Patience of Job. 'S'all in the Good Book. And let us not forget Moses, who spent many years in search of the Holy Land…" This outpouring was brought to a merciful if embarrassing finale by a very loud belch.

Anastasia cast a contemptuous look down her thin nose at him; and I overheard Bascombe turn slightly towards me and mutter, heard only by myself and the Reverend: "Aye, well, Moses had a better class of material to work with. And *he* knew how to maintain a bit of *discipline.*"

The chaplain, hearing this, turned slightly toward the Major. "Ah yes," he wheezed with relish, *"discipline."* And he set what passed arguably for his jaw, and smacked his hand into his fist in that familiar and most violent of gestures, as if imagining with pleasure another delectable flogging. Bascombe merely turned away from him with a sneer.

McMurdough had not heard this little exchange, merely nodding to Blythe as he returned doggedly to his own favourite – indeed, well nigh his only – topic of conversation.

"Patient, yes," he nodded. "Quite. A virtue I have had much cause to exhibit recently. I was, er, telling you about my new Spanish ram. Fine masculine fellow, but for some reason he does appear a touch reluctant to er…"

His voice and rather unsavoury illustrative gestures of husbandry, and his wife's long-suffering rolling of the eyes at this, faded to the background as I followed the angular form of the morose Major making his way slowly away from this group and toward the card table. There I fancy I glimpsed Dr Mountfort now frowning down at an apparently much diminished pile of coins and rather apprehensively picking up his next hand. Bascombe now stood behind him, observing the play with some degree of disapproval.

I dropped my battling eyes downwards to my glass. It was the latest of several and would not remain full for long.

When I had drained it, and lost count of how many more had followed, I became hazily aware that Felicity, Ffeffington-Weekes and some others were now also in the room, chattering away in a separate cluster over by the window. I glanced furtively towards my chirping cousin, well able to imagine, even through the haze of my diminished senses, those eyelashes fluttering at the pretentious popinjay's every ludicrous word.

I reached once again for the decanter and was about to refill my glass, when a gentle voice said nearby: "Don't you think you might have 'ad enough, Doctor?"

I turned towards Polly, whose face loomed as a pinkish smear above me.

"Well… you know…. spirit of the occasion and all that… great explr… exo…" I concentrated hard and finally succeeded: *"…explorations…"*

"Well, she's very pretty and no mistake," Polly said softly, with a glance toward's Felicity's distant form. "But I fear you might be wastin' your time there, sir."

I followed her gaze, struggling but not quite succeeding in focussing upon its object. "Ah well," I slurred bravely, "she's not the only fish in the tree. Bird in the ocean. Er, bush in the…" I looked back to my glass and held it up to the light. "… mm. Not a bad drop."

Another figure now loomed near my shoulder. I drew back slightly, startled, as Polly turned to the newcomer.

"Oy! Shameless!" she demanded in a loud whisper. "I been lookin' for you for ages. Where 'ave you been?"

"Just... down at the stables," came the familiar brogue, with a note of self-defence. "Seein' a man about a horse."

Polly raised an eyebrow - or I assume she did, since my vision had long since passed beyond the discernment of any such detail – and fired back: "Aye, stealin' a horse, more like."

"Now why would yer be sayin' somethin' like that?" he cast back, indignantly. "I'm a reformed man, I keep tellin' yer."

"Oh yeah," she smirked, "an' pigs might fly. Anyway, I think it might be time you helped the good Doctor back to his quarters - 'e's had one too many."

"One?" whispered the stablehand rather loudly, casting his expert eye over me. "He's completely..."

"Hist!" said Polly, raising a finger to her lips. "Don't let the Guv'nor see him like this. Or the Major."

They looked across the room, to where I was very dimly aware of my uncle and Bascombe engaged in apparently heated conversation, the Governor presumably imposing upon his subordinate another of his tirades. At the thought of those, my head began to swirl ever more rapidly.

"I'll take him back to the stables for the night," suggested Shameless; upon which I became aware of being hauled less than gracefully to my feet. "Come on, Your Overdoneship," he cooed, "upsy daisy now".

"But the night is yet young...", I blurted, gesturing wildly. "I have not yet begun to fight... for my Queen of the Desert... *Unhand me,* if you please, Mister Ticket-of-Leave..."

It was to no avail. My limbs were well past complying with the commands of my brain. I could do little more than mumble incoherently as I was dragged unceremoniously away. My last memory of the great banquet was of a kindly though still blurred figure shaking her sandy head and returning to her work among the tables.

The card game continues late into the night. Gambling in its various forms is already rampant in the colony. Dr Mountfort is clearly no stranger to it – though as with so many things, experience doesn't necessarily equate with skill or success. In fact, his pile of coins has dwindled to almost nothing – much of it having gone into the visibly swelling pile of the chuckling Captain Partridge.

Mountfort has now called for a short break, during which he's locked in an earnest conversation with Major Bascombe - who he knows to be a man in good position to bolster the doctor's imperilled gambling stake with a promissory note for a quantity of liquid currency.

Having first quickly established that the Governor is not nearby, Bascombe reluctantly consents to being drawn behind a bookshelf to discuss the matter.

"Come now, Bascombe, you know me to be a man of my word," implores the portly medic. "Just a small additional advance, man – nothing I shall not be able to repay with ease, and at a reasonable rate of interest, once my luck has turned."

The Major returns his urgent look with one eyebrow skeptically raised. *If only luck could be turned as easily as that. If it could be*, he broods, *my own life would be a very different story.* He begins to calculate what the return will be upon the steep rate of interest he intends to extract from the good doctor. At this moment, Partridge pops a cheery face around the bookshelf.

"Come on, Mountfort old chap," he chirps. "We're waiting for you."

14. THE PLOT SICKENS

Early next morning, dew sparkling upon sturdy tufted grass. Shameless and Jacky are already down in the paddock behind the stables, with Carmel.

The native is involved in the serious business of giving riding lessons to the Irishman, who's struggled at first with the daunting task of hauling himself up onto the creature's back. Once there, it's a matter of balancing his not insubstantial frame on its hump and wrapping his legs as far around as possible. Jacky laughs while quietly giving tuition to his scrambling cohort.

Shameless is growing quite fond of Carmel. He's warmed to her affectionate though somewhat stubborn nature. She's not unlike meself, *he smiles:* may be hard to shift, but at the same time, not easily panicked. Not like the horses — they're taking their time getting used to her, although there are early signs of progress in that department.

One particular attribute of the desert beast for which the stablehand has great appreciation is that a camel doesn't need to be shod. For that blessing, he's even forgiven her the earlier bite.

In the back of his mind forms the vague thought that at some future point, perhaps if more of the creatures were brought in, one could fairly soon begin to organise races between them. And wherever there could be races, he thinks, there could be a spot of wagering organised. And, he thinks, I'm just the man to do it.

Perhaps with this prospect in view, slowly Shameless begins to respond with more skill to Jacky's chuckling tutelage. Carmel in turn becomes more responsive to his commands.

So too, a friendship between the jovial Irishman and the laconic native is growing steadily. They begin to understand, even anticipate, unspoken signals in the dart of an eye or the shrug of a shoulder. We underdogs, thinks Shameless, have got to stick together, an' that's a fact.

All in all, the three of them are getting on like a house on fire. But now the sun is climbing inexorably higher into the piercing blue sky.

"Well…" sighs Shameless at last, "I'd best be makin' a move to revive the good doctor."

At this, Jacky mimes drinking and staggering about. Now it's the convict's turn to laugh, at a most convincing impression.

Within an immense gaudily panelled courtroom with a high, vaulted ceiling, I stood grovelling before the bench. Towering over me, my uncle, the judge, bellowed abusively down at me, vilifying me utterly for the wild, irresponsible and generally disgraceful nature of my prosecution of the case. My wig slipped to the floor and I grovelled bare-headed and helpless before the onslaught.

In the dock, the prisoners – including the McMurdoughs, the Reverend, Bascombe, Mountfort and several others – leered and guffawed with each judicial insult, and finally burst from their confinement to advance upon me and haul me bodily into the dock they had just vacated. There I cowered in terror as my uncle solemnly placed a huge black cap upon his head and pronounced sentence of death upon me. At this point the whole shipboard courtroom began to sway and buck, the crashing of the waves rising to join the crescendo of cackling and screeching laughter; as a hooded executioner of oddly familiar bearing lumbered slowly towards me, his corpulent shadow swallowing my pathetic and screaming figure…

At this point I did not so much wake as cringe pathetically into the daylight, suffering not so much a hangover as a landslide. As I half opened my eyes and blinked, the floor steadied and my true surroundings came shafting harshly into view. Land ho again, thank God.

I at once perceived that I was lying upon a rough bed at the stables, my ears filled with the vociferous crowing, cooing and cackling of the local birds.

Waking to the sound of birdsong may sound very pleasant and romantic in theory; in practice it is an altogether different experience when one is in such a state that any sound at all represents an affront to the sanity. When, in addition, the varieties of feathered creature prevalent in one's part of the world include robust varieties armed with screeches and guffaws that would wake the dead, the result is that the one so awakened comes to the immediate conclusion that he would indeed be better off dead.

And what was that shadow spreading ominously across the floor? I moaned and looked up – but drew back again immediately as a formidable shape loomed up, larger than life, in the dazzling doorway. I had thought I was now firmly back in the conscious world – but was this not my executioner, come to drag me back into the nightmare from which I had just escaped?

Then, in a relieved instant, I recognised the figure as none other than Seamus Halloran.

"Ohhh, God," I managed. "What time is it?"

"Eleven hundred hours, Your Slumbership, or thereabouts."

I started up with a shock at this. "Eleven h… Good God, I'm supposed to be at the surgery!" With this I flung myself from the bed and lunged to my feet.

The combined effect of several sledgehammers having simultaneously and comprehensively shattered my skull at this action, I clutched my head with a bellow of pain and collapsed back onto the bed, moaning piteously. I fancied I heard the infernal birds now cackling even more loudly at my distress.

"Easy does it, there, sir," said Shameless with an understanding grin. "I've already sent word surgery would be postponed to this afternoon, because of the good doctor bein'… indisposed."

"Ah. Er… thank you." I was much relieved at this, and lay back to watch him shuffling about at his work.

The more I had observed him in this, the more I had come to realise that neither his working space nor his manner of utilising it were by any means as chaotic as they had first appeared to be. Though not immediately apparent, things were set out in just such a way as to somehow bring the required tool or gear within easy reach at the very moment that it was required. The ropes, chains, blocks and tackles hade been deliberately placed so that they were close at hand to be utilised for raising and moving saddles and heavy tools, saving any unnecessary strain upon the back.

It was hardly what one would call neat, but there was a definite method in this madness. Bascombe may have routinely dismissed him as "lazy"; Halloran preferred to describe himself as merely being economical with his precious energy – and so it appeared. The overall impression of him at work was of a rather stout vessel meandering with seeming aimlessness about the ocean, but somehow managing to find at each accidental port of call precisely the required provisions to continue its leisurely voyage.

At this point in my train of thought I paused with a shudder and realised that, especially given my current state, imagining any kind of seafaring was unwise in the extreme; and the immediate nauseous rush was heightened by Shameless, as he shuffled over to the fireplace, coincidentally launching into a hearty whistle of some inane sea shanty.

"I'm sorry," I almost gasped, "would you mind… not doing that?"

"Doin' what?" he asked blankly.

"The whistling."

"Ah. Sorry. We Irish, you see, are a very…"

"… very musical people," I cut him off irritably. "Yes, so you said. And I look forward to hearing convincing evidence of that theory on some future occasion. But not now, if you please."

"Oh dear," he chuckled. "We are sufferin' the after-effects, aren't we." He dipped a mug into a pot upon the hearth. "Here, try some o' this." And he thrust the mug of steaming coffee into my hands.

After expressing my gratitude for this, I took a tentative sip, wincing now not so much at the headache as at the memory of the previous night.

"Oh, God. Was I terribly embarrassing?" I asked.

"You don't remember?" he asked with a grin.

"Nothing much at all past the truffles, I'm afraid – and rather too much before."

"You were certainly well medicated, Doctor. Don't think I've seen a man in such a state since the old days back in Dublin," he grinned to himself with nostalgia, "drinkin' with the likes o'… Michael Flanagan an'… Padraic Malarkey. And they were no amateurs, those two, to be sure."

This brought something else into my head – besides sledgehammers. For a moment I wrestled with it, frowning silently. I took another sip and said, perhaps in partial contrition for my earlier musical insult, "Excellent coffee."

He nodded in modest acknowledgment as my impaired grey matter continued to grapple with something that had rung a bell in what he had just said. Slowly, the hazy recollection began to assert itself.

"Padraic Malarkey, you mentioned…? Now where have I seen *that* name…? Ah yes." It came back to me now – the surgery, the anatomy book, the page fluttering onto the desk. "On… a grant of land."

"You what? Padraic Malarkey?" said Shameless with a distinct note of surprise.

"That was the name on the title. Ticket-of-leave man, I suppose, like yourself…"

He looked at me quizzically. "On a… land grant, you say?"

"Yes, I believe so."

"An' how did you chance upon this document?" he inquired.

"Well, as it happens, it was in my surgery. Fell out of one of Dr Helfcott's textbooks. Padraic Malarkey – that was the name, no mistake. Must have dropped his deed while visiting the late doctor. Or given it to him for safekeeping. I'd forgotten all about it. Didn't think it could be of any significance."

Shameless, however, pupils flickering intensely, now spoke slowly and with some deliberation, like a prosecuting attorney closing in for the kill. "An' just exactly when would this… land grant have been made?"

"I don't know, I think it was dated … perhaps, yes, a year or two back."

He was looking at me with the strangest expression. I was in no state for riddles and cross-examination. "For God's sake, man, what is the matter? It's only a plot of land."

He waited for a moment and then said quietly: "The only *plot* Padraic Malarkey occupies… measures six foot by two. I could show it to you. He died more'n five years ago."

My brain was not ready for this. Not ready at all. I merely stared at him, blinking like some nocturnal creature caught in the too harsh light of late morning.

Felicity Blythe is back in her room, back in her favourite spot in front of the mirror, indulging her endless concern with her own image. She peers at her face and prattles on, as the long-suffering Polly strains to lace her into an elaborate whalebone corset.

"Such extraordinary bravery! Single-handedly discovering the Inland Sea and opening up the Great Interior."

"So he said, Ma'am. Several times." *Polly is entirely secure in the knowledge that her sarcasm will pass unnoticed, as does almost everything she says or does. No match for the mirror. Her mistress twitters on without so much as a heartbeat's pause.*

"And think of it: poor Maximilian actually went for six weeks without so much as a... dressing table or a crystal glass."

Polly, under her breath, to herself: "'Maximilian', is it, now!"

"I would have gone mad. Imagine – not a looking-glass in sight."

Expressionless: "Horrors."

"He was <u>so</u> impressive," *Felicity bubbles onward, the corset now firmly in place.* "Even that old cow Anastasia couldn't stop staring at him and grinning like an old witch. I'll wager she'd love to get her ageing claws into him. I do find it ever so undignified when a woman throws herself at a man so shamelessly."

The poor maidservant bites her tongue with some ferocity and almost chokes to stifle the tremendous guffaw that threatens to explode from within. She affects a sudden bout of coughing to mask the superhuman effort.

"Look out, you silly girl," *scolds the young mistress.* "Take care or you shall squeeze the breath out of me!"

In me dreams, thinks Polly. In me dreams.

Still within the stables, I watched Shameless as he returned to the business of repairing saddles and other riding gear, though now frowning with contemplation of this new mystery.

I was dressed now, and sitting up upon the end of the bed. Thanks to the coffee I felt marginally less deathly, and my thoughts had by this point regathered sufficient coherence to prompt the obvious question: "So why would the Governor issue a grant of land to a dead man?"

Shameless turned. "If he did."

"Well, he signed the grant, I saw his signature." This was a quite distinct memory. There it had been, my uncle's florid hand very clear at the bottom of the page: Sir Henry Blythe, Governor of His Majesty's Colony of Port Fortitude.

The stablehand gave a dismissive shrug. "His signature'd be on everything, doesn't mean he reads 'em all. With all due respect to the Governor, I don't think he knows one convict from the next. They all…"

"All look the same," I concluded the familiar sentence. "So you said. The er, tailoring."

He ignored the inconvenient historical allusion. "Yes, well the Governor probably just signed this grant in among a whole pile o' papers."

I followed his train of thought. "Papers drawn up by, and brought to him to sign by…?"

"Well now," he said with a slow nodding, "that'd be our Major Bascombe."

"Ah. Bascombe. Yes." I met his wry and disapproving expression at the utterance of the name. "But of course, you'd have no great liking for him, now, would you."

"Nor he for me," he responded defensively, and jutting out not merely one chin but both of them, in what he undoubtedly fancied was a gesture of heroic national defiance, "nor for any Irish political prisoner."

"Political prisoner?"

"Indeed so, sir. Swept up as I was in the brutal repression o' the Great Rebellion o' 1798."

"Oh, is that so? But er… " I feigned surprise, rather wickedly enjoying this moment, "do correct me if I'm mistaken, Halloran, but I had understood that you were transported here… for forgery."

He drew himself up at this, bristling – which was not difficult, given the amount of bristles upon his chin – and responded with the utmost sense of wounded dignity: "Forgery? Sure an' that's an unkind word for a man merely doin' his bit for his poor impoverished country by… increasin' the money supply a little."

Not bad, I thought, not bad; but he had not finished yet, sweeping on with grand rhetoric: "After all, haven't the greatest Irish heroes been branded as thieves, at one time or another, all the way back to Finn McCool?" (I believe that was the name he mentioned; I rather suspect that I may not have spelled it correctly – but it is quite difficult enough to decipher the utterances of the Irish without having to spell them properly.)

Shameless shook his head sadly. "Nothin' changes. Plus la change, as the French say."

"Indeed. C'est la vie," I agreed, suppressing the threat of a smile at his misquoted French and shaking my own head in feigned sympathy. "Well then… what now?"

As if to calm his bristles, he rubbed them, eyes sharp in thought. "Well… I imagine you might be wantin' to find out a tad more about how these land grants are made. But we'd best be careful about how you do it."

"Ah, so we'll be careful, but er… I'll be doing it," I clarified.

His look was indulgently forgiving in the extreme. "Well of course. How else could it be?"

I had no answer. How else indeed.

15. FURTIVE ENDEAVOURS

I must admit, it could have been done a great deal better - but I was, after all, by nature a straightforward sort of chap, and quite inexperienced at this kind of devious play-acting.

The Major was in his office at the barracks when I rapped lightly upon the door.

"Come in," came the less than welcoming response. I did so, to find him labouring unenthusiastically at checking rows of figures in the columns of a large ledger-book.

Attempting a breezy nonchalance I began: "Ah, Bascombe. Glad I found you here. I wanted to ask your... advice on something."

As he looked wearily up at me, I saw he appeared even more tired and haggard than usual – as though he had not slept in days. The already pronounced lines of worry had become even more so. Even the sideburns had lost something of their bearing, lying lank and limp against his sallow face. Perhaps he too had suffered after-effects from the banquet, though I had not noticed him drinking to excess upon that occasion. Not that I would have noticed any such detail towards the latter part of that fiasco.

"Aye, what is it?" he asked flatly.

"Well... I was just wondering how one might go about applying for... a land grant."

He sneered, eyes firing up immediately, throwing back his head and thrusting out that imposing chin. "Good God! In the colony barely a month, and already you're after a nice plot for yourself."

I hastened to explain myself, the feigned nonchalance immediately surrendering to genuine embarrassment: "Well, that is, not straight away, I… I was… merely curious about the er, the process…"

He rose, and paced jerkily around me, launching into another of his bitter outpourings.

"Know how long I served here, in this far-flung hellhole, before I was given a land grant? Eight years. And when they did, it was halfway down a steep gorge covered with impenetrable jungle." He looked down his quivering chin at me, eyes burning. "All right for some though, I suppose, when they've got the backing of their wealthy families, eh?"

"I was merely wondering," I mumbled, chastened, "how it's done, the er, the granting of land. Just in case… er, for the future, you under…"

"Well, since you're determined to know," he cut in, "the Governor makes the land grants. People apply, I collate the paperwork and the Governor decides. If it was up to me, I'd say you can wait in the queue like the rest of us. But I suppose your family connections will help to bypass the dreary formality of that process, won't they?"

I opened my mouth to speak but the words had run dry.

Tom Quayle and Geoffrey Bascombe are not aware of it, but at this moment their conversation is overheard. Outside the window, Anastasia McMurdough has walked quietly up, having tethered her horse a little further away. She wants to be quite certain the Major is alone before discussing the rather pressing matter that she wants to take up with him.

She steals soundlessly up to within earshot of the window. Hears Bascombe's raised voice and realises that someone else is with him. Bends over slightly and draws up as close as she dares alongside the casement, listening beneath the open shutter.

As the conversation draws to its awkward close, her face darkens with deepening concern.

She bites her lip, ponders the significance of what she's overheard. Annoyed shake of the head. Does he not suspect what may lie behind this inquiry?

This will not do, determines Milady. No indeed, this will not do at all.

In the Governor's office, Blythe is pacing in his usual manner around the seated, abashed, hand-wringing form of the Reverend Staines. The Governor's tone is severe.

"Altogether too many reports of corrupt behaviour getting back to the Colonial Office. Misbehaviour on the part of our leading citizens, including clergy, reflects badly on the colony as a whole."

"Yes, but... I guarantee Your Excellency," protests the good Reverend, giving the hands a good wring, "I've done nothing wrong."

The Governor is incredulous at this. "In God's name, Staines - or at least wearing his collar - you were seen for the second time this month, emerging from the Marlin Rouge! An establishment whose existence is unofficially tolerated purely to meet the... er, baser needs of the soldiers, pending the arrival of larger numbers of more suitable female company."

"Ah, now that's just it, Excellency," *interjects the Reverend. Fiddles with the collar.* "I was merely... inspecting the facility, to ensure it was not tempting any personages of higher position."

The Governor raises an imperious eyebrow and smirks: "Apart from your own, er... missionary position, you mean?" *He allows himself a moment to savour his little joke, then moves without further ado to the conclusion of this audience:*

"Yes, well let me make it plain, Reverend: I am instructing you to carry out any future such 'inspections' in the company of a suitable witness - and during daylight hours."

The Reverend, chastened if not chaste: "I shall do the best I can, Excellency."

And the icy response: "I had an uncanny feeling that you were about to say that."

Late that night, all is quiet within Government House; until, in a darkened hallway, comes a sound of muffled footsteps.

Around the corner comes creeping a shadowy figure. Cloaked and furtive. Carrying a small partly-shielded lantern.

The figure moves silently towards a doorway, steps chosen carefully to avoid the tell-tale creak of loose timbers. Now the hooded one reaches the door, looks down at the legend: "Governor's Adjutant - Private".

Now the head lifts, and the light from the lantern catches the face beneath the hood.

It is the maidservant, Polly Dawes. She looks about, lips clenched in tension. Turns back to the door.

It cannot be avoided, she determines. Get on with it, girl, no time to waste. Glancing around furtively once more, she takes out a small sliver of metal and bends to the lock, picking it with some skill. After only a moment the door opens and she slips quickly inside, closing it quietly behind her.

Inside Bascombe's darkened office, Polly goes to a large wooden filing cabinet, sets the lantern down upon it. Takes out another metal device, opening the cabinet with equal deftness.

Now she rifles quickly through some files, looking for something. No, this won't do, she thinks. Nor that one. Then: Ah now, perhaps more like this...

She takes out the file, goes to the desk and spreads it out. She smiles grimly. Ah, she thinks, now this is just the kind of thing we'd be lookin' for. Yes, he'll be pleased. Now if I can find more of...

What's that? She stops dead, heart to mouth, listening keenly. Footsteps are approaching along the hallway. Quickly Polly covers the lantern, bundles up the file and crouches behind the desk with it.

She starts to imagine the consequences of discovery. Gawd, oh dear Gawd. At the very least I'll be consigned to the backbreakin' hard labour o' Norfolk Island for the term o' me natural. It's too awful to contemplate for more than a moment, and she suppresses these thoughts by biting her lip hard, almost betraying herself by crying out in consequence. Same lip she bit so hard to mask her hilarity at her mistress's hypocrisy. And now twice as painful. Eyes water uncontrollably.

A tense moment passes. Mercifully, the footsteps subside. Until at last, all is silent once more. Polly waits a moment to steady her breathing before slowly returning to the cabinet, uncovering the lantern and reaching into the trove of secrets. The illicit search continues.

16. TAKEN FOR GRANTED

"Is it very much farther, do you think?"

I must have sounded rather irritable, and so indeed I was. Shameless and I had ridden for goodness knows how many miles to the west, over rolling hills and through low scrubland and thickets of dry forest towards the mountains.

Now we had come into a slight clearing, from which towered a large, overhanging sandstone rock of eerie bearing. I fancied from somewhere I could hear the music of strange Pan flutes or some such. I shook my head – this was presumably some lingering after-effect of my hangover.

I was startled by a movement and turned to see a kangaroo bounding past and disappearing into the scrub. This was one of the many strange creatures that inhabited these parts: a mouse-like head superimposed preposterously onto a dinosaur-shaped body that somehow managed to leap about through the undergrowth as nimbly as a gazelle.

Wherever one looked there seemed to be another odd mutant creature: luridly-plumed squawking parrots with absurdly tufted combs; squirrel-like beings with enormous staring eyes swinging from improbably spindly tails; and perhaps most bizarre of all, a tree-dwelling native bear. This last-mentioned Antipodean idiosyncrasy blinked lazily from the lofty foliage, languidly scratching its tufty ears as it pursued the slow and imperturbable mastication of every last leaf in the surrounding treetops – so much of which these beasts consumed that they looked far too bloated and soporific to retain their hold upon the branches, moving only to lumber slowly up and down from one meal to the next.

No creature so preposterous could ever have survived but for the virtual isolation of this continent for so many eons having deprived it of any serious competition. In this continent so far removed from the treadmill of naturalistic development, the order of the day appeared to be, one might say, survival of the fattest.

Something about this scruffy, pot-bellied, furry-eared, leisurely creature reminded me of… what was it? My still less than fully functioning brain struggled to make the association, until:

"Not far now," said Shameless, looking up from the map, grinning and scratching his ear as he munched lazily on a twig. "Head still a bit sore, Your Hungovership?"

I merely grimaced, partly to mask the impulse to laugh at my companion's now all too evident resemblance to the creature I had been pondering.

"Ah well, could be worse, sir," he said jovially. "At least it's not a sea-going vessel."

"It feels very much the same in all significant respects, particularly its refusal to stand still."

"Well, if it's any constellation to you," he offered, "I'm not exactly findin' it comfortable meself, what with me own disablement." He indicated his rear. "But we do have to find out who's actually in possession of Malarkey's plot."

"Yes, yes. Of course," I agreed. "Let's just get there quickly, shall we."

We rode on, finally emerging from the forest onto a hillside. Shameless pointed towards a very pleasant and mostly cleared pasture dotted with sheep, grazing comfortably upon its patchwork of grasses.

We rode across toward this pasture, and looking down the hill, we spied a convict farmhand at work on a fence – which for some reason been bolstered on both sides with stands of some kind of prickly bush.

Shameless hailed the farmhand as we approached. "Hoy there!"

The fellow looked up but said nothing as we reined in our horses and came to a standstill alongside him.

"Top o' the mornin' to yer," Shameless offered.

The farmhand merely nodded and turned back to his fencework with a gruff "Aye."

It was my turn to stamp my authority on the situation. "You er, work on this land, my man?"

"Aye."

"For who?" Shameless asked.

"The boss", answered the erudite fellow helpfully.

"And who would that be?"

Still not looking up: "The landowner."

"Of course," I exclaimed, becoming annoyed at his uncommunicativeness, "but what is his *name*, man?"

Finally the farmhand looked up at me, squinting suspiciously. "Who wants to know?"

Shameless looked meaningfully at me.

"Er… I do," I said, attempting to sound commanding. "Dr Quayle, Colonial Surgeon."

The farmhand was so impressed at this that he was driven to respond with his characteristic effusiveness: "Aye."

Then Shameless added pointedly: "And *nephew to the Governor.*"

Ah, now this appeared to have rather more impact. "Oh," he said, "Well then." He paused and considered. Then he turned slowly, looked me in the eye and said: "Land belongs to… Colonel McMurdough."

Now it was the turn of Shameless and I to lose our tongues. We pivoted slowly towards each other and exchanged the most interested of looks.

Anastasia's eyes flash imperious emerald. Hisses. "He wanted to know <u>what</u>?" The maidservant whispers again. Milady's jaw sets grimly, every strut in that patrician bone structure at full strut.

She remembers with deepening suspicion what she has overheard at Major Bascombe's window.

Finally her husband, the Colonel, is unable to resist noticing that something is happening outside the engrossing world of his dinner plate. He looks up, spluttering with his mouth full: "What's that? Anything the matter, my dear?"

Antarctic smile meets his gaze. "No, dear, it's… nothing. Just a small domestic trifle. No need to trouble yourself."

He has long since learned to trust all such matters to his efficient spouse. "Ah." And with no further word or thought he returns, satisfied, to his meal.

Anastasia sits and ponders, grinding her teeth in bitter consternation. Infernal complication. After coming halfway around the globe to begin afresh, it seems we are still being pursued. Is there to be no end to it?

"All right, so let me get this straight," I said, leaning my elbows upon Shameless' rough table that evening, and summarising what we had gleaned from our mounted expedition. "A valuable plot of land is granted to a dead man, then ends up in the hands of Colonel McMurdough."

"A profitable transaction for all concerned," Shameless judged, then adding darkly, "Except Malarkey."

He did not look up from dismantling some mechanical object – a pastime oft indulged in his spare moments, he'd say, "just for the pleasure o' seein' how they tick."

"Indeed," I persisted. "But a transaction presumably set up by Bascombe and gratefully received by the McMurdoughs."

"Aye," he agreed. "An' poor Helfcott was unlucky enough to tumble to it, by comin' across a land grant made out to a man he knew was dead, because he'd signed his death certificate."

"Mm," I nodded, pursuing this deductive path. "So he thought he'd better tell someone about it."

"And that someone," Shameless concluded dramatically, looking up from his dismantling at last, "was none other than the Governor's Adjutant and keeper of the colonial land titles: Major Geoffrey Bascombe. A logical enough person to confide in, or so it seemed. But in goin' to Bascombe, the good doctor had signed his *own* death certificate."

I nodded gravely, then turned directly to him. "You seem to know a great deal about the process of grants and such."

"Well now," he said with a twinkle, "that'd be because I've been doin' a bit of research, sir. And to that end, I've taken the liberty of engagin', you might say, a rather useful assistant on our… er, on *your* investigation."

And at this he turned towards the doorway and called: "You can come in now, Polly."

And in strode the familiar ruddy maidservant. Shameless rose politely and said "You've met Polly Dawes, Doctor…"

There she was, all dimples and smiles, just as I'd last seen her at the… well, I thought, that memory was best left where it lay. I rose, slightly startled at her arrival, but Shameless sought immediately to reassure me: "It's all right, Polly is entirely trustworthy."

I whispered aside to him: "How can we be sure?"

"Oh, I've known Polly for years," he said aloud, smiling. "We go back a long way."

For some reason I could not help muttering, in mimicry of my uncle: "Mm. Not sure I find that particularly reassuring."

Polly grinned in response to this, and assured me that "I'd trust Shameless 'ere with me life," but then she added with a twinkle, "though not necessarily wi' me purse."

Shameless cast her a brief indignant frown of momentary offense before explaining: "Polly's been… takin' the opportunity to examine a few of Major Bascombe's documents in his office at Government House."

"But surely they would be kept under lock and key!" I protested.

At this Polly grinned, a little embarrassed. "Well, I'm good with locks. See, that's this 'rehabilitation' for yer – you learn new skills. Dawes is the name, openin' doors is the game."

I started to chuckle at this, then attempted rather awkwardly to cover my reaction by attempting a slightly disapproving frown - the effort of which was utterly wasted by both of them ignoring my response altogether.

Polly's face was turned towards Shameless, who was in full stride now. "Polly's discovered some very interestin' papers locked away in the good Major's cupboards. There's been all manner of shady dealin's emanatin' from that little quarter."

"Includin' lots more dodgy land deeds," she nodded, turning back to me, "an' also a great many convict death certificates, filed away but never sent home…"

"But why, for Heaven's sake?" I asked her.

"So their land could be re-sold – at a tidy profit."

"And," Shameless added, "as a nice little bonus, their rations can go on bein' drawn from the Mother Country – also to be re-sold. The profit goin' presumably into a certain Adjutant's pocket. And I'll wager there's been a lot more o' the food supplies creamed off besides, judgin' by how much thinner the convict rations have been gettin'."

"And all these documents," said Polly, "with the Guvnor's signature on 'em…"

Shameless tilted his head. "If indeed it *was* his signature. Could have been forged."

"Oh," I could not resist interpolating at this, "and would that be the… political, or the non-political kind of forgery?"

He did not miss a beat. "That depends whether you're on the winnin' or losin' side o' the transaction," he twinkled. "But no, in this case I wasn't the forger. This is well out o' my league." And he added quickly, "Even if I'd still been in that line o' work - which I'm not, bein' as I said, doctor, a reformed man."

"Anyway," Polly interrupted firmly, apparently not wishing to dispute that problematic assertion at this juncture but preferring to return to the present point, "the Guv might very well've signed 'em all, but without bein' aware of what he was signin'."

"But Bascombe knew, to be sure," said the stablehand pointedly.

I nodded. "Yes, that does appear an inescapable conclusion," I agreed; then to Polly, "And you say this has been going on for… how long?"

"Years an' years," she replied, "with no-one any the wiser, it seems."

"Until poor Helfcott stumbled onto it," said Shameless.

"And for his troubles, earned himself an assisted passage – straight off the end o' South Head," concluded Polly.

As if to punctuate this, from somewhere in the distance came a low rumbling of thunder.

"And let's not forget," added the Irishman, "Bascombe was aware of the doctor's morning ride routine – and would have been in a better position than anyone to… creatively abbreviate the girth."

At this we all exchanged significant looks. Clearly, everything in our investigations was pointing inexorably toward the embittered Major.

17. DEAD RECKONING

At this very moment the Major in question rides up to the barracks. Dismounts, tethers his horse. Casts a weary eye toward the heavens.

In the twilight, the first glimmer of evening stars has been swallowed whole, the sky brooding under a massive head of stormcloud rearing up from the south. Aye, this'll be a big one, thinks Bascombe. Best get inside quickly.

He heads for the door, half smiling in sour observation: Into each life, a little rain must fall. In my case, he sniffs with bleak resignation, it'll be a bloody downpour as usual.

As he reaches the doorway he stops suddenly, hearing a noise. His lean figure tenses. Someone has whistled - distinct enough sound, quite unmistakeable even over the approaching rumble of thunder. He looks around, peering into the near-darkness.

"Who goes there?" he demands loudly. No answer. Clutching his musket, he takes a step towards the darkening bushes, squinting.

A scuffling in the undergrowth. He points his gun. "Come out of there, or I'll shoot!"

He looks fiercely down the quivering chin. Another rustle. Who or what is emerging?

He takes a half-step back. A flash of lightning and the figure sliding out of the shadows is clearly illuminated to him as if in the beam of a lighthouse lantern.

Bascombe's expression changes at once to one of familiarity. In fact something more – almost pity. A slight sneer crosses his face. He lowers the gun to his side.

"Oh, it's you," he drones wearily. "Well, I'm ready for you." And with this *he takes a short and deliberate pace towards the figure, almost as if a single mournful step lifted from a funeral march.*

Suddenly there is a short, sharp squelching noise. Bascombe grunts loudly, eyes staring in shock. His chin quivers one last time, the sidelevers shivering in the gathering breeze. Then for a brief instant there is almost the suggestion of a wry smile, and with it a final snort of derision for... more or less all of it, really. Is that it, then?

The eyes glaze over, and he tumbles into the welcome embrace of darkness.

Another flash of lightning, accompanied by a loud clap of thunder. Then the raindrops begin to fall, dark as fine rum and heavy as gold coins.

Like a bull into a china shop, Shameless came careering into my surgery without knocking, as I was in the midst of salving yet another predictable infection. Outraged, I shouted: "Halloran, what do you mean by bursting in? Can't you see I'm with a patient...?"

"I'm heartily sorry, your Doctorship," he blurted breathlessly, "but you... you'd better come with me, sir!"

"I can't just..."

"I'm afraid it's very urgent," he insisted, eyes wide and blinking like a startled native bear caught in the sudden light of a lantern; and he added for good measure one more "Very."

"Oh... all right." I turned apologetically to my patient. "I'm sorry, Mr Flaherty, I shall call for you again later in the day, and hopefully we may complete your treatment then – *without interruption,*" I added with a pointed glance at Shameless as I ushered his disgruntled compatriot to the door.

Then I returned to confront the intruder. "All right, now, this had better be good. What in heaven's name is..."

"It's Major Bascombe, sir. He's been found just outside, in the bush. He's dead."

I gulped. "Good Lord."

Numbly, I followed him out of the door, into the pouring rain, and across to the edge of the nearby scrub.

A crowd of soldiers, Captain Partridge among them, was gathered around the body of Geoffrey Bascombe. He was on his back, a long carved wooden spear protruding from his chest, his red coat soaked with rain and faintly stained with the darker red of his blood, which had spread with the rainwater into a vast pool about him. His eyes, drained at last of all resentment, stared blankly upwards into the deluge. His *bitter experience* was indeed at an end.

The familiar rush of revulsion gripped me and I fought hard to prevent myself surrendering to the wave of nausea. Without a word I took a deep breath, gritted my teeth and bent slowly to examine the body.

After some minutes of grisly, gut-churning analysis I stood up, dripping and quite ashen-faced I am sure, just as the Governor rode up. With him was Dr Mountfort, huffing in disgust as he dismounted, appearing less than pleased at having been hauled away from his comfortable fireside – most likely another dinner gathering and cards – and into the midst of this dreary, drenched and deadly tableau.

Uncle dismounted, handed the reins to a trooper and strode forward, one glance more than enough to confirm the awful reality.

"Merciful Heavens, it's true then. Have they caught the accursed native who did this? Where's Colonel McMurdough?" This was met with blank looks from the troopers.

"Get him here at once," he barked to Partridge. "I want every native in the area rounded up immediately and put in the stockade." Partridge issued hasty commands to a couple of troopers who dashed off to seek the Colonel. Blythe turned back towards the body.

He shook his head, face grim. "Most unfortunate." A brief pause. He shook his head again. "Poor Bascombe. Not well liked, perhaps - but whatever his failings, a soldier of the King."

He turned to me, his tone businesslike. "Quayle, I want you to make your examination and settle up all the paperwork as quickly as you can. No point in letting this cause any more alarm than it needs to."

"Me? But w-why not Dr Mountfort, Excellency?" I stammered, gesturing towards the corpulent medic, who was now giving the late Major a most cursory examination. He did not even bother even to lower his ample frame towards the prostrate form, but merely prodded lackadaisically at the corpse with one tooled boot as he somehow managed to defy the drizzle by deftly refilling and lighting his pipe. All the while he was chatting cheerfully with the shrugging Partridge and the other troopers, none of whom appeared greatly upset by Bascombe's demise.

"Surely," I persisted, "Mountfort would be the more senior…"

Uncle cut me off irritably. "Dr Mountfort is far too busy attending to the health of the officers and settlers. This is a straightforward administrative matter, quite properly the duty of the colonial surgeon. See to it, man, and without delay."

"I shall do the bes…" I started to say, but very quickly changed tack: "Er, yes, very well, sir."

The Governor nodded, turned and strode at once to his horse. He mounted, dragging his diminutive frame up the side of the beast and into the saddle with singular purpose, and rode off without further word, Dr Mountfort beside him. Having presumably satisfied himself by his rather less than rigorous examination that yes, the Major had indeed shrugged off this mortal coil, the portly doctor was now almost visibly itching to return to the far more congenial business of fireside and cards.

We turned to watch as Partridge and the other soldiers now lifted Bascombe's body and carried it away, back into the barracks - leaving Shameless and I standing there together, side by side in the drenching rain.

There was a long silence before I spoke, quietly, over the intermittent thunder. "Well. So much for our prime suspect."

"Ah well, look on the bright side, sir," he entreated.

I looked at him blankly, unable to imagine that there could possibly be any such positive aspect to such an awful event.

One corner of his mouth curled up sardonically. "At least it can't have been an Irishman - he wasn't *murdered in his bed.*"

18. ALL HELL

A loud crack of thunder awakens Polly Dawes in her tiny bedroom alongside the kitchens of Government House. She looks out the window at the flashes of lightning. Rain sheeting down.

Above the downpour she hears a loud noise in the courtyard below and peers down to see the Governor dismounting, men rushing out to help him and lead the horse away. All of them are shouting and slipping around in the mud and behaving as men generally do.

What on earth are they doin' out there, on a night like this? My Gawd, she thinks, men are such fools, as a bunch. They make such a noisy fuss and they rush about tryin' to make 'emselves look important, but when you look at it, they get so little done properly.

Like my poor late husband, she thinks ruefully (and not for the first time). All I ever wanted from him was just to earn us a modest livin'. Just so's we could get a small shop goin', dressmakin' or some such, and rent some rooms near the river – an' maybe start a family. But he had to go and get such lofty ideas into his head about becomin' such a big shot, makin' lots of money, real Mister Bleedin' Big he was goin' to be.

An' what did it get him? Hanged – and me transported. Men.

Well, she promises herself, I won't be makin' a mistake like that again, not in an awful hurry. No more of that kind, men too big for their boots.

She thinks now upon those men who have shown an interest in her since she arrived in the colony. It's not like some 'aven't shown their intentions – mostly of the less honourable kind. Her chin sets firmly in bitterness at the unpleasant recollection of what she had to do to defend herself against that vile fellow who tried to…

Ah, she recalls, but then good ol' Shameless… what would have become of me if he hadn't borne witness to it bein' done in self-defence? An' if that wasn't enough, he somehow managed to produce no less than seven other "witnesses" to the event – an' not one of 'em, she chuckles, who was actually there. How he managed to connive their testimony I never did find out – no doubt by bribery or bargainin' of one kind or another. Well, he may be a rogue, thinks Polly, but deep down he knows what's right. I owe him one, an' no mistake.

She ponders further, with an inward grin: Always wondered whether he was just settin' himself up for a bit of… No, she shakes her head, I mustn't always think the worst of men. There's some of 'em that's not so bad, an' Shameless is one o' those – well, mostly, underneath like, as much as can be expected.

An' I must admit, there's one or two others is not so bad either. Like poor old Doctor Helfcott. A good man he was too, kind like.

An' o' course there's the new one. The young doctor. Ha! "I'm Tom!" An' then he tries again: "Tom Quayle!" No, "Doctor Tom Quayle!" and then he finally gets to it: "The governor's nephew!"

She chuckles again for some moments at the memory. Well, she concludes, <u>he</u> at least doesn't have too many big ideas. And then upon further reflection: Not sure whether he has too many ideas at all, come to that. Makin' such a fool of himself over… well, men are so stupid, aren't they – always fall for the pretty ones with the trim figures and the big battin' eyelashes, that gets 'em every time. Then they wonder why they finish up gettin' 'emselves into such pickles.

And as for whether he has the ticker to make a go of it out here, to handle the hard life… well, she concludes, we'll just have to wait and see on that score. Still, he does have that kindness in his eye…

She yawns, rolls over. Listens for a while to the rain pelting onto the roof. Drifts slowly back to sleep. She will not remain so for long, before being reawakened - by the two men most recently in her thoughts.

The storm rages on, the sky screaming, lashed again and again by wildly jagging cat-tails of light, the thunder banging and cracking fit to shake the fragile colony to its fledgling foundations. The wind cackles with cleric-like glee at this relentless flogging of the firmament, the trees whipping and snaking, large branches wrenched loose and flung through the snarling sky to smash gaping gashes in ramshackle rooftops.

What follows is a twisted Antipodean rendition of the parable of the Three Little Pigs.

The poorest porkers in this version: the convicts who have built their dwellings from fragile fronds of cabbage-tree palm, lashed together with vines and scraps of fabric. These hovels are ripped to shreds in no time at all by the howling, gnashing wolf, their occupants sent scurrying to the shelter of more established neighbours who have constructed their cottages from boards wattled with small twigs and plastered with clay. Some of these are sturdy enough to withstand the battering of the storm, but some in turn begin to crack and collapse under the onslaught of wind and rain.

At this point, the little piggies within should by rights run squealing to the generous shelter of their astute sibling with the house made of bricks.

Bricks, however, are in short supply in this setting of the parable. And routinely reserved for little pigs possessed of sufficient quantities of currency, whether of the solid or liquid kind, to purchase materials for the construction of a decent dwelling. Unfortunately these little pigs are all of the free-settling variety, and fancy themselves rather too far up the social pecking order. Or perhaps simply too fearful to allow little porkers of a convicted felonious kind to share their law-abiding dwellings, even briefly and under such extreme circumstances.

So at this point the piggy parable breaks down – as a growing flock of convict families now seeks urgent refuge in the only other available haven: the Church. This edifice is soon crammed full to creaking overflow with wet and disshevelled parishioners, constrained to endure a hastily improvised and characteristically slurred sermon from the Reverend Staines upon the wrath and vengeance of the Lord and the well-deserved destruction of Sodom and Gomorrah.

While this reading is well assisted by the theatrical crashing and flashing of the heavens, the Reverend's rendition itself is so melodramatic - and so clearly affected by intake of liquid currency - as to pass well into the realm of ham-acting; so much so that many of the flock are soon in some doubt as to whether it might not be preferable to head back outside to brave the elements, rather than sit like wet sardines enduring the liquor-scented fire and brimstone belching from within the House of God.

And the performance will suffer even more from a further unforeseeen complication. One dwelling which has suffered severe damage is the Reverend's beloved Marlin Rouge. Its walls stand up well enough but its roof is ripped rudely off just as if it were one of the occupants' bodices, and flung wantonly into the nearby scrub. The provocatively half-clad occupants of the nefarious establishment flee shrieking to the Church, where they arrive with impeccable timing just as the Reverend reaches the climax of a fiery passage pertaining to the sins of the flesh — a reading rendered completely incoherent by the harassed cleric's eyes now falling almost constantly upon the dripping, corseted figures of these distinctly fleshly sinners. No Christian martyr in the Lion's Den was ever forced to endure such adversity. Nor ever handled it with such distinct lack of grace.

Outside, the rain comes down in rivers which it seems will never be stemmed. But then, slowly, the thunder fades and the downpour begins to subside.

Some hours later, several troopers bustle up to the barracks complex, with a dark figure secured by chains trudging heavily between them.

Jacky stumbles slowly along in the darkness and the now steady drizzle. Eyes glaring straight ahead, blinking and fearful. Jostled by the jeering troopers.

Colonel McMurdough and Captain Partridge emerge from the barracks to meet them. A few words pass between the uniformed men. The chained prisoner is bundled inside.

They push him roughly into a cell in the stockade, where he staggers against the far wall and slides to the floor. The troopers lock the door with a loud clang.

Jacky sits up and rubs his bruised shoulder. Dripping and shivering, he stares at the wall facing him. The more he stares at it, the more it seems to close in around him. He buries his face in his hands.

"He was the only native they could find," explained the exasperated Shameless. "Rest of his people avoid this place like the plague."

In the predawn darkness we three bleary-eyed figures trudged through the mud towards the stockade, Halloran clutching the fateful spear, Polly and I on either side, talking in tense whispers.

"I know," Polly remembered ruefully. "Bascombe used to go out like clockwork, once a month, to 'keep the colony safe' by roundin' 'em up. Only problem was, he never seemed to actually find any. So him and the soldiers would come trudgin' back, Bascombe would growl about havin' chased 'em away, about how they didn't dare show their faces on account o' bein' such cowards – but if you ask me they just knew better than to 'ang around this dump."

I nodded, still barely awake, blinking through the damp darkness towards the barracks. I had been shaken rudely awake in my own quarters there by Shameless, who was spluttering with outrage at news of Jacky's arrest. How he had learned of this in the middle of the night, I did not even bother to enquire, having long realised that when anything of significance occurred, Shameless would inevitably and smartly come to know about it by means of his elaborate and ubiquitous network of listening ears and watching eyes.

Stumbling by candlelight into my clothes, I had followed him to Government House where we awakened a grumbling Polly and headed back with her to the barracks.

Despite the reassurances of Shameless, I had remained slightly apprehensive of widening our circle to include Polly, and had taken the liberty of inquiring further into her background. I had heard of her widowing and her transportation here, resulting from smuggling activities. I was appalled at the accounts of her attempted rape by another convict, in the course of which she had despatched her assailant with a kitchen knife, but was ultimately acquitted on the ground of self-defence. Following this, she had attained her ticket of leave and been taken on by my uncle as maidservant to Felicity – and had performed this duty, by all accounts, without blemish.

She was, fair to say, highly regarded in all quarters as a woman of some character, despite her earlier transgression. I must say though, looking across at her now, I did feel just slightly uneasy at the graphic descriptions of what she had done with the kitchen knife.

This, however, was not the only source of my uneasiness at this juncture. I was also becoming more and more concerned about the possibility that we might all be in danger, that someone might even now be watching us, waiting for a chance to…

I hazarded a quick glance behind us, half fearing to see another spear come whizzing towards us out of the darkness. There was nothing there, however – well, nothing, at least, that could be seen through the drizzle.

We had arrived now at the barracks complex, where we proceeded to the stockade, and were met there by an armed guard. I confronted him rather tentatively, introducing myself as he squinted through the gloom to recognise me: "Dr Quayle, colonial surgeon. I must interview this prisoner in connection with the death of Major Bascombe."

I held up the paper carrying the official seal of the Governor. The guard peered at this, then shifted his gaze uncertainly onto Shameless and Polly.

I quickly reassured him: "These two are material witnesses in the case. I shall take responsibility for them." He appeared rather reluctant but nevertheless consented to stepping aside and admitting us to the cell.

Jacky stepped forward to greet us, relieved to see friendly faces but obviously in great fear, his eyes constantly moving around the walls as if they were falling in upon him. Meanwhile Shameless was also casting his eyes dartingly around the room in their usual instant absorption of detail. It was like watching two pairs of mosquitoes chasing each other around a flame. My sleep-deprived head started to spin and I was obliged to cast my own eyes to the floor to re-establish my equilibrium.

Jacky listened keenly as we explained what we knew of events. Silently he examined the spear – and after only a moment of this he concluded with certainty: "Know this spear well. Anyone throwing… SWOOSH!" (he mimed the action) "… spear himself… very neatly through foot."

"What are you sayin'?" Polly demanded, frowning.

"Not made for throwing," he said. "Only for ceremonies, that one."

Ah, I nodded, now this helped to explain something that had unsettled me since I had examined the body. "I *thought* the angle of entry of the spear was a little odd," I said. "Up under his ribcage, instead of down through the torso as it would have been, if thrown." Shameless nodded slowly and keenly at this, eyebrow raised.

"You seem very sure about this spear," said Polly to Jacky.

The latter shrugged. "Should be - carried back here myself. Exotic native item 'discovered' by Cap'n Great Explorer."

I almost shouted with vengeful glee: "Aha! Ffeffington-Weekes! It was *his* spear! So *he's* our killer. I knew he couldn't be trusted, with all his Great Explorations and his Inland Seas and…"

But Shameless flung up his grimy palm to forestall my energetic, though perhaps not entirely dispassionate, line of deduction. "Ah now, hold your horses, Doctor. I saw all those spears, in the Ballroom. They were all left there on display, after the banquet."

Polly nodded, perceiving the significance of this. "So anyone with access to Government House could have got hold of it," she concluded.

Damn, I thought, glowering. Almost had him promoted, as it were, from ass to assassin.

"We'd better make some more inquiries," Shameless decided; and turning to the prisoner: "Jacky, I thank you - you've been of great assistance."

"Don't worry – we'll get you out," promised Polly with a smile of hearty and dimpled determination.

And Shameless observed wryly: "First Aboriginal to live in this colony, and you've already achieved a hundred-per-cent imprisonment rate."

Keen now to add my own reassurance to the unjustly imprisoned fellow, I threw in: "Well, fear not – we shall soon have that back to zero."

Jacky merely winced, putting his hand meaningfully to his throat. "Mm", he grunted. "One way or another, eh."

I opened my mouth but then shrugged and smiled stupidly at my gaffe. There was nothing more to be said.

We turned to go – but Jacky held up his finger and said suddenly: "Oh, one more thing. Possibly important." We all turned back sharply to face him. He went on:

"Night of great banquet, observed Major Bascombe… near stables. In…" he grinned, "secret couples' business. With… " he lowered his voice to a whisper, "Lady McMurdough."

"I told you about that choice little rumour, weeks ago," said Polly to Shameless as we headed slowly back through the slush from the barracks towards the stables.

"I hadn't forgotten. I was merely uncertain what credential to attach to it - given the vagrancies o' the colonial gossip mill."

"Seems the gossip mill had it right, for once," she said. "Apparently that little liaison's been goin' on for some weeks."

I stopped still, enthusiastically grasping this new whiff of progress. "Well," I ventured, "*there's* a motive for us. Spurned affection. What if Lady Anastasia was rejected by the late Major? Hell hath no fury like a woman scorned."

" 'specially a woman like her," added Polly. "She'd be up to a damn site more fury than most."

"Or here's another thought," Shameless barrelled in: "what if Bascombe was *blackmailing* her? Can't imagine the Great Lady consentin' too happily to partin' with any of *her* precious booty. Much more likely to take preventory action against the blackmailer."

"Or what if *McMurdough* found out about the adultery?" I posited, trumping him, or so I believed. "Hell hath no fury like a husband horned," I said, making with my hand the twin-pointed sign of the cuckold.

Polly commented on this with a smirk, "Not sure he'd have the wit to understand what he was seein'."

"Oh, I don't know," chortled Shameless crudely, winking and nudging me uncomfortably in the ribs. "To be fair to McMurdough, he does know his *animal husbandry,* if nothin' else, ha ha!"

Polly frowned at him in mild rebuke. "Well, you're not wrong though," she admitted to me, "that's another motive that's got to be worth thinkin' about."

"It seems there are motives popping up all over the place", I said. "There's still the whole Malarkey land transaction, and the role of the McMurdoughs in that."

To this, Halloran added: "And let's not forget all the other gossip doin' the rounds, about the McMurdoughs an' their indubious histories."

"Indubious?" I asked, in both factual and lexical query.

"Lady Anastasia goes on at great length about how she comes from a long line of European nobles," Polly explained, "an' they say she's squirrelled away lots of plundered loot – though if that's true, no-one quite knows where she keeps it."

"And as for her husband the Colonel," chipped in Shameless, "it's said he also came here on the run - from some questionable business transactions, which certain associates of his back in England might still be harbourin' more'n a slight grudge about."

I raised my eyebrows and nodded. It seemed wherever one turned, past and present skeletons were creeping out of their shadowy closets to point their bony fingers at the good citizens of Port Fortitude.

As if reading my mind, Polly added with her wry grin: "Like they say, doctor, there's only two reasons for someone bein' in this colony: either you been sent 'ere by force, or you're runnin' away from somewhere else."

I looked away for a moment at this, uncomfortable in the realisation that in my own regard, both of these motives were at least arguably true.

"In any case," said Shameless slowly, "I think we'd best be takin' a closer look at our grand pastoral pair and their dealin's. Polly me girl, I think you've got a tad more diggin' to do."

"Oh, look here," I protested at once, turning to him. "Is that really necessary? I mean, it's a dreadful risk, and I do fear Polly has been pushing her luck already."

"Well," he shrugged, "how else do we go about getting' the information we're needin' on the land transactions? Should we be frontin' up to the Guv'nor again, perhaps, an' askin' him?" he smirked.

"But what if she's apprehended? Think of the consequences," I pressed.

"We'll just have to cross that bridge when we come to it," he replied doggedly. "It's a risk we've got to take. Polly's a free agent in the matter," he said, looking respectfully at her.

I turned away, frowning. A convict servant, caught in the act of rifling through Government House files. This would be a capital offence. To save her, I would have no choice but to front my uncle and take the full responsibility upon my own shoulders. I would have to admit outright that I had ordered her to do it – and why? Because I was pursuing a line of inquiry into the dealings of the Governor's most senior officer, against my uncle's own express command.

And I would have to take the awful consequences of that admission.

I imagined the scene – stripped of my position, sent home in disgrace. The mere thought of that interminable sea voyage by itself was enough to send my stomach into a flat spin, let alone the contemplation of what would await me upon my return home.

"Don't give it a thought, Doctor," came Polly's voice behind me. "I'll take care. I'm good wi' not getting' caught."

I turned to meet her twinkling eyes, and that cocky grin with its reassuring dimples might have almost begun to calm my tumultuous vitals - had she not added with a note of concern, confirming my already well developed fears:

"It's *you* what really needs to take care. You're the one who's known to be doin' the investigatin'."

And Shameless added, nodding in grave agreement: "That's right. An' we still don't know to what degree your predecessor's fate was due to his position as colonial surgeon."

"You havin' taken on that role," added Polly, "might well put you in danger for the same reasons."

"All in all", concluded Shameless, "if I were you, doctor, I wouldn't be goin' into any dark places on yer own, not till all this is cleared up."

I gulped at this, paling visibly, I am sure, by several shades.

19. THE FINAL PIECE

In the hallway of Government House, at night, the Adjutant's office door opens very slowly. Again the hooded face of Polly peeps out. Again she casts an eye quickly in both directions, emerges furtively - bearing a bulging sheaf of documents which she stuffs inside her cloak and waits. Again looking about with great care and listening for several moments for any approach. There's none, so she scampers quickly off down the hallway.

As she heads towards the door of her own bedchamber she stops suddenly, hearing something. A loud, definitely human – and unless she's much mistaken, female noise. To be more precise, a sob. It comes from the kitchen, its doorway next to her own room.

Polly slips quickly into her bedchamber and stashes the papers out of sight. Then she returns to the kitchen door and opens it quietly. Enters, soundless, tentative, curious.

The large kitchen is being mopped by a quietly blubbering young convict woman, who she recognises. Polly moves towards her, speaking gently. "Sadie! Sadie Potts! Whatever is the matter with you, girl?"

Sadie returns her gaze tearfully and dumbly, eyes large, choking back a sob.

My uncle was most assuredly not happy. He drummed his fingers impatiently upon his desk, colour rising in his jowly face. He ran his hand with irritation through his thinning thatch.

"But look here, Quayle, I asked you to conclude the inquest *quickly*. Surely it can be no more than a formality. We have our murderer, we have our murder weapon."

I knew I had to speak quickly, to have any chance of firing out sufficient convincing information before he cut me off. "But sir," I began with a rush, "it couldn't have been the native. It was Ffeffington-Weekes's, um, a trophy, from the Ballroom, left in the Exped… er from the Expedition, in the Ballroom, left in the… anyone could have…"

It was a disaster. What confounded quirk of nature is it by which the dire need for communicative speed and coherence operates in precisely inverse proportion to one's capacity to summon these skills when thus needed?

Uncle banged his fist upon the desk. "For God's sake, *stop raving*, man! It's cut and dried and I want it *finalised by the weekend*."

He rose and walked around the desk. "I shall announce it at the Anniversary Hunt. A most important occasion, marking ten years of the colony, and a suitable opportunity to publicly put this matter to rest, and to reassure the settlers that Port Fortitude is safely governed under the firm rule of British law."

He turned to face me. "At the banquet upon the conclusion of the hunt, you will make a brief report of your findings, and I shall announce that Bascombe's murderer is to be swiftly and finally dealt with."

I opened my mouth, aghast at the implications of this and desperate to get through to him; but no words emerged, and rolling his eyes, he swept his hand at me, cutting off my threatened objection.

"Come come, Quayle. Grow some *spine*, for God's sake, man. He's merely a native, and a lawbreaker who would suffer precisely the same fate under his own people's justice."

I slumped in wordless desperation as a knock at the door prompted the usual bark: "Enter!"

The door opened and Colonel McMurdough entered, carrying a large hessian sack.

The Governor, apparently glad of a chance to close off any further attempts by me at quibbling with his commands, greeted the Colonel: "Ah, McMurdough. Just the man."

The Colonel appeared rather taken aback to see me there. He put down the sack, and he and Blythe exchanged salutes.

The Governor explained. "Colonel and Lady McMurdough are in charge of the arrangements for the hunt." He turned to the Colonel: "So then – how is it all coming along?"

"Most satisfactorily, sir," came the starched reply. "The South Head site is being suitably prepared – and as you are aware, I have brought a quantity of foxes out from England to foster the noble sport of hunting in the colony."

"Ah yes, so you said," rejoined the Governor, tossing his head back and raising an eyebrow. "Forgive me, however, for remaining skeptical of the capacity of foxes to survive in these conditions. After all, what are they to *eat,* man?"

"Ah yes, well, I've er… thought of that as well." And with this, McMurdough reached slowly into the sack and pulled out by the ears a large rabbit.

The Governor and I exchanged a look, he frowning.

"Rabbits, man?" boomed Blythe. "Much too dry for rabbits. They'll never take on here!"

The rabbit, hanging by its ears, blinked dumbly at us.

"Whatever foresight may be demanded of us here, I can't see us ever having the need to build any quantity of rabbit-proof fence in these climes," chortled the Governor.

Now it was I who did the pacing - around the interior of the stables, before Shameless and Polly who were seated glumly upon the stablehand's bed, lit by the flickering candle.

Following my convict cohorts' warnings about my safety, I was now ensconced in the stables almost permanently beyond nightfall, sneaking over here in the twilight and not daring to return to my own quarters until I could scurry back there in the safer light of daybreak.

I had to admit I had come to view the stables as a home of sorts. I had even become accustomed to the pungent smoke arising from the pats of cow dung Halloran used to repel mosquitoes. At least they were not as foul as the trooper's pipes.

"Well," I warned, "unless we can track down the real murderer by the weekend, poor Jacky will hang for it – and most likely me as well, should I utter any further protest about the matter."

Shameless gave a lopsided grin of exasperation, shaking his head. "Problem is, all the evidence points to the victim bein' his own murderer. If anyone else'd been killed, we'd have *known* it was him."

There was a distinct double-take from Polly and me at this gem of Irish logic, together with a certain amount of eyebrow-related business.

Shameless scratched his head distractedly with a saddlery implement, frowning and flexing his woollen brows. "I just know we can't have been that far off the mark. There's gotta be somethin' more, somethin' we've overlooked…"

He went over to the enormous sheaf of papers and began to scour them, looking for goodness knows what item of corroboration.

Polly sat back. "Well, look… there may be somethin'."

We turned to her. She raised her hand slightly, as if warning against putting too much store in what she was about to convey.

"It's only an outside chance, but… in the kitchens last night, I came upon Sadie Potts all a-tearful, an' I asked her what was wrong, and it turned out she was gettin' all weepy about Bascombe. She used to share his bed, you see – before Lady Anastasia got 'er fangs into him. Anyway, I managed to get Sadie talkin' about him… and… "

"Yes?" I prodded.

"Well, she was talkin' of him keepin' things to himself, an' she said she once saw him writin' in this… little book. Like a… diary or somethin'… hid it away and got quite angry when she asked to see it."

"A diary?" I frowned. "No such item was found in the search of Bascombe's quarters."

"Maybe *I* should have a look," she offered. "I'm good at findin' valuable items – specially in other people's houses."

I grinned, eyebrow raised. "Another of your 'rehabilitation skills'?"

She returned the grin with an impish twinkle and our eyes held just for a moment. She appeared now, I had to admit to myself with some slight sense of unease, a good deal less plain than when I had first encountered her.

It was now late evening. The three of us had scoured Bascombe's quarters for almost two hours.

I sat back dejectedly upon the bunk. "Absolutely nothing."

"Can't understand it," said Polly, scratching her head. "Should 'ave been 'ere somewhere."

Shameless came in. "No luck round the outside?" I asked him hopefully.

A mournful shake of his head. "Not a sausage."

I sat back, leaden. "So the sum total of what we have now, amounts to one theory – your latest offering, Shameless, ingenious though it may be, but supported by about enough substantial evidence to have anyone advancing it immediately slapped into the brig, or worse."

Shameless bridled. "Look, it's got to be," he insisted. "Where there's smoke, there's got to be…"

However, I was spared a repeat of his outlandish theory by Polly, who was staring hard at the chimney.

"Fire", she completed the sentence very quietly. Then at once she moved to the hearth and lay down on her back upon it, looking up into the sooty recess. She reached up and scratched about for a moment, giving a small cough at the soot falling onto her face.

Then her eyes widened and she exclaimed "Ha!"

Slowly she retrieved a blackened, cloth-wrapped item. We rushed to her as, with the greatest eagerness, she began to unwrap it.

"Will yer look at that," said Shameless, awestruck.

"Well, well," I murmured, grinning. "A veritable bloodhound."

"But without the obedience, I suspect," added the Irishman with a twinkle.

The sooty cloth fell away in Polly's hands to reveal a small writing book. She opened the front cover.

"Polly, you're a genius," said Shameless reverently; and he added with a nod: "An' I should know."

I leaned over her shoulder and began to read aloud. "Journal of Major Geoffrey Bascombe. A true account, written in my own hand, to be read only in the event of my death…"

We looked at each other. I gulped and continued to read.

It was a bleak and almost gothic narrative, its manner plodding and formal. It was certainly not written in a style calculated for successful serialisation in a popular periodical. Nevertheless its content was from the first page utterly engrossing, unfolding as it did the inexorable steps towards the demise of its narrator. A demise, with hindsight, surely courted - and perhaps by the end, one suspected, even knowingly sought.

Within minutes my voice was cracking with shock as the truth emerged, clear and cold and utterly incontrovertible. As I reached the journal's key point of revelation, I became aware that Polly was gripping my shoulder. I did not attempt to remove her hand, merely paused and looked across at her. Our eyes met, hers bright and brimming.

Then I looked over at Shameless. A grim smirk of satisfaction had spread across his face.

"I knew it," he said quietly. "Had to be." And indeed we could not disagree: his far-fetched theory had turned out to be in all respects, as they say, "bang on the money".

The following morning I walked nervously up the street towards Government House. All around were groups of convicts scurrying about engaged upon various duties, mostly involving extensive reconstruction work necessitated by the considerable damage wrought by the storm.

I was taking care to remain in full view. I had to admit that I was now most acutely conscious of movement all about me, especially of any sounds from behind.

As I neared Government House I encountered Colonel McMurdough emerging from therein. I waited until he had moved down the street a little and then stepped forward to intercept him. Upon seeing me he stopped dead, looking startled, and avoiding my gaze, quickened his step and moved to continue past me.

I stepped quickly across in front of him once more and said: "Good day to you, Colonel! A moment, please!"

He stopped still, and stood blinking at me, warily. "What is it?"

"I need to talk to you, Colonel. If you don't mind."

He appeared most displeased at this prospect. "Look, I am really quite… busy at the moment, perhaps another…"

"It is a rather serious matter, I'm afraid", I interrupted. "And rather urgent." I lowered my voice. "It pertains to the death of Major Bascombe. I must insist that you accompany me, please."

His eyes shifted, then he drew himself up and consented with considerable reluctance: "Very well, if I must."

"This way, Colonel, if you please." I indicated the pathway towards the barracks, and waited for him to move ahead of me. He walked stiffly, glancing frequently over his shoulder at me in a manner perhaps even more apprehensive than my own.

20. TALLY HO

Back in the frill-throttled bedchamber of Felicity Blythe, the usual primping and preening - aided by the usual long-suffering maidservant. The latter struggles to maintain any degree of concentration on the work, mind and heart bursting with a complexity of anticipation, excitement, and the gravest apprehension.

"Oh, I do love hunting, don't you?" chirps Felicity, utterly oblivious as always to the sensibilities of any but herself. "So exciting - all those strong, able-bodied men in their smart jackets…"

"Aye, all that blood…" adds Polly, barely managing even mock enthusiasm. *Not at all surprised at the ironical tone passing several miles above the lady's head.*

"Yes, it all adds to the general atmosphere, doesn't it. And of course", she smirks coquettishly, "Maximilian will be there…"

And Polly responds through clenched teeth: "Of course he will, milady."

The aforementioned Maximilian is at this point down at the stables, engaged in his favourite activity: lecturing. In this case his singularly unenthusiastic captive audience is Shameless, who stands desperately affecting mannerisms of respectful attentiveness. And looking on, the imperturbably munching Carmel.

"You must, therefore, make sure the beast is properly groomed," the Captain intones down his nose toward the stablehand. "I want it in tip-top condition, so that I may use it to illustrate some of the more dramatic moments in my great expedition, the full details of which I have not yet shared with the colony."

Lucky colony, thinks Shameless. Perhaps seeking more conducive communion, he turns toward the munching dromedary with affection. "She'll be lookin' like a beauty queen, sir. Won't you, Carmel?"

The Great Explorer's nose turns up with disgust. "Do stop calling it that."

In the Government House kitchens, Anastasia McMurdough sweats profusely under her high-buttoned collar. She hisses commands to Mavis, the senior cook, watched from a short distance away by Milady's husband, who wears a strange and - even for him - unusually distracted look.

"... and the second course," the Great Lady pronounces, "is to be served in the marquee, exactly one half hour after the first, and please be sure it is made exactly to the specifications I have laid out..."

"Yes, Milady," smirks Mavis aside to a colleague. "I believe you've... 'laid it out' very well."

Suppressed giggles from several of the convict women, quickly silenced by Anastasia's lacing looks about the kitchen. She stares hard at the cook. Sets the jaw in cement. Lashes down the anger. Turns with an enormous show of restrained dignity to the Colonel.

"Come, Montague," she instructs.

She takes his arm and they walk stiffly away, he frowning distractedly. She darts a glance towards him, wonders for a moment what preoccupies him. And then concludes, anything at all would preoccupy a mind such as that.

Aware of the suppressed titters continuing to ripple among the servants, she urges through clenched teeth: "Smile, my dear, smile," and in exasperation: "What is the matter with you?" And adds almost in reflex: "Never mind, rhetorical."

He attempts the faintest of smiles towards the kitchen staff, avoiding the eyes of his wife. She continues in a precise whisper as they walk with controlled slowness along the hallway. She is determined not to let this exasperatingly soft spouse go to water now. Not now that they have come so far and put so much behind them.

"It is imperative", she lectures him imperatively, "that we continue to present a respectable face to the lower classes, Montague. We must be seen to be above *responding in any obvious way to any salacious gossip that may come to our notice – gossip put about, I have no doubt, by those jealous of our position in the colony."*

The broad, nondescript face responds, rather stonily: "No doubt."

At this precise moment someone else is seriously doubting the security of his position in the colony. Or for that matter, anywhere.

Jacky the native peers from his cell window, between the bars, into the barracks courtyard – to see the platform and scaffold which are permanently established there. This hasn't been used for some time – but now a trooper is engaged in the macabre business of attaching a length of stout rope, a noose in its end.

Jacky gulps, sweat breaking out on his brow. He staggers backwards onto the bench and sits, rocking slowly back and forth, head in his hands.

"Let's go through it one more time, then," said Shameless, as Polly and I leaned forwards over the table. "The hunt is over, the dignitaries are all seated in the big marquee…"

I nodded. "All, er, seated, yes." I was relieved that our plan provided for me to arrive immediately after the hunt itself, since I had no desire to subject my weak stomach to the grisly demands of that event. As Shameless and Polly had pointed out, it was in any case safest not to provide an opportunity for the engineering of any untoward "accident" which might easily be arranged to befall me during such an activity.

Shameless now continued: "… An' the Governor will call on you to deliver the findin's of your inquest into the death of Major Bascombe."

"Yes… and er, where will you be?" I inquired nervously.

"I'll try to stay within sight of you, Doctor," he promised, "but as I've already explained, I can't be too close. You can see what would happen if there was any suggestion of you bein' in league with convicts. Your credulity'd be shot to pieces."

"Yes, that's true." And I added quickly, and particularly to Polly: "Er, no offence."

"None taken. Just don't forget those documents," she cautioned.

"Yes. Er, I mean, no. Of course. The er, the documents, no. Er, yes."

She smiled indulgently at me. " 'Ave courage, now, doctor, it'll go all right", she said kindly. And she added another of those winks, of which I had to admit I was growing rather unnervingly fond.

"Could I make just one more suggestion, sir…" ventured Shameless.

"What's that?" I narrowed my eyes slightly, having grown a more than a little apprehensive about suggestions emanating from that dubious quarter.

"Might I suggest that just before you ride out to South Head, you calm your nerves just a smidgin with a small shot o' that excellent medicinal spirit you've recently transferred to the second top shelf o' your locked cabinet. Just a small one, mind."

I nodded. This did seem a good idea. But then I turned to him, slowly, through narrowed eyes.

"Wait a minute. How do *you* know that's where I've moved it to?"

He grinned and shrugged non-committally. Polly glanced disapprovingly at him.

"Well," he blustered, " it'd be the obvious spot for it. You wouldn't want to let just *anyone* get hold of it, now, would you."

South Head towers massively over Port Fortitude's main bay. Its rolling heathland surrounded by a thin lip of dense scrubby bush, hardy eucalypt and windblown ti-tree forming a tightly-knit windbreak. On the other side of it are those high sandstone cliffs directly overlooking the ocean, which froths and snarls against the fallen boulders under the menacing vigour of a rampant mid-morning sun.

On the occasion of the Port Fortitude Tenth Year Anniversary Hunt, a large ornate marquee has been erected at the top of the hill, near the edge of the band of bush bordering the cliffs.

From somewhere comes the unmistakeable piercing hoot of a hunting horn.

At the verge of the scrub, a hessian sack is opened and a red fox at once rushes out. It darts a look around the alarmingly unfamiliar terrain before recognising the all-too-familiar barking and baying of approaching hounds and plunging off without further delay into the undergrowth.

There are loud cries of "Tally Ho!", and thundering hooves among the barking of the dogs. Various riders dash off in pursuit over the heath, bursting in and out of the scrub where they imagine their quarry to be.

Among the hunters: the Governor, Colonel McMurdough, Captain Ffeffington-Weekes, Captain Partridge and Dr Mountfort, all exhibiting varying degrees of difficulty in negotiating the dense, tangled bushland. Somehow whenever a hunter is about to urge his mount into a canter, its progress is checked by another steed. Or a hound rushing in front of it. Or some scrap of unexpected flora.

Meanwhile several ladies, riding sidesaddle in long dresses and ornate broad-brimmed hats, are attempting to upstage each other in as ladylike a fashion as possible. Anastasia and Felicity are taking this as far as actual - though subtle - attempts to unseat each other by sudden equestrian manoeuvres. Their struggles are soon interrupted by the Great Explorer, who comes riding gallantly up, leaping over a fallen log to impress Felicity, and almost falling from his horse in the process.

Sitting upon my bunk, I pulled on my boots whilst my stomach performed somersaults.

I was not at all sure we would be able to bring this to a satisfactory conclusion. The risks, it had to be admitted, were considerable. I bit my lip as the vision once again materialised of my mother, back in England, little imagining the risk of complete disgrace now being willingly contemplated – nay, indeed actively courted – by her errant offspring.

Still, having come thus far, it was evident there could be no turning back, and no other course of action presented itself other than the one upon which we had determined – though whether the word "we" was strictly accurate, whether I had really had much say in the matter or had merely been browbeaten into this nightmare by my two convict accomplices, I was not at all certain. Paradoxically it was only with their assistance that our desperate plan might have any chance of success, however slim.

It appeared the thing would have to be done, and better sooner than later. Yes, I determined, best get it over with. Now is the moment, I thought. Yes indeed, I decided, let us without further…

I fancied I heard a burly sailor encouraging me to attempt the rope ladder before the next change of tide.

I took a deep breath, gathered my wits, rose and hurried out through the surgery. A few steps outside I remembered Halloran's advice, paused, darted back within, and found the medicinal spirit – on the second-top shelf of the locked cabinet, just where the rogue had so suspiciously known it was.

Smiling and shaking my head at the thought of his remarkable cheek, I took a swig. And then, yes, one more – a good generous one, capable of easing the internal knots just slightly.

Then I was out of the door, stuffing a large wad of documents into my saddlebag.

Suddenly there was a noise. I turned with a start. It was a low scuffling, in the bushes, just over there near where Bascombe…

I gasped, veins turning to ice. Then almost choking with fear, in a mouse-like whisper, I demanded: "Who… who's there?"

I took a small, tentative step towards the rustling.

Suddenly, the bushes burst apart and a large dark grey form burst forth.

I screamed and raised both hands before me as … what I now realised was a kangaroo landed with a thump a few paces away. The startled creature darted a single panicked glance in my direction and was off in an instant, two bounds carrying it away into the undergrowth.

I cursed loudly to myself and stood trembling for several minutes, panting heavily.

Then, slowly, I turned back to my horse, darting nervous glances over my shoulder as I did so. Making more than one attempt at the saddle before attaining some measure of security thereon, I rode – or perhaps more accurately, floated numbly - off towards South Head.

Back at the headland, the hunters are faring no better than before. There are several minor collisions and falls. Fortunately these result in no serious injuries – at least, none to anything more than pride.

Captain Ffeffington-Weekes picks himself gingerly out of a clump of prickly bushes, where he has just slid gracelessly from his mount after failing to negotiate a tricky bend in a bush track. The Governor, McMurdough and Partridge ride up, pistols gleaming in their waistbands.

"Still no sign of your blasted fox, McMurdough," complains Blythe. "Off chasing your rabbits, I have no doubt." *He motions to McMurdough and Partridge who dismount and stride over to the fallen explorer, assisting him to his feet.* "Come on, there, Captain. Up we get."

"Damned vegetation," *grumbles the latter, picking prickles from his breeches.* "Sticks out all over the place – not like our decent British forest. The horses are quite unsettled by it."

"Not to mention the riders – eh, McMurdough. Ha ha." *The Governor flicks this towards the Colonel but the latter does not pick up the barb, looking immediately away from the Governor - only to find his eye in contact with the imperturbable smile of Captain Partridge. McMurdough immediately avoids this as well, his gaze darting somewhere off into the bushes as if in pursuit of the elusive fox.*

Ffeffington-Weekes meanwhile steams into another of his interminables. "I recall during the expedition, there was one particularly gruelling stretch where I had struggled my way through a particularly treacherous patch of undergrowth…"

Partridge starts to chortle at this, coughing to cover it up and muttering "excuse me" *behind his hand; and the Governor interrupts quickly to prevent the unfolding of yet another explorer's epic:* "Yes, well, never mind, Captain – we shall soon have it all nicely cleared – just like England, what?

"Well then," *he says, dusting his hands together briskly,* "we'd best call it a day, gentlemen – the banquet awaits us; and certain… sombre formalities must, I am afraid, be observed."

Ffeffington-Weekes now back in the saddle, they move off, the Governor leading the others up towards the marquee.

There, Polly and Shameless observe their arrival. Carmel stands not far off, near the edge of the bush behind the marquee, awaiting her role as an unwitting prop in yet another Ffeffingtonian narrative epic.

Polly is becoming more than a little concerned. "Luncheon's about to be served and no sign of the doctor," she hisses to Shameless. "What's keepin' him?" She squints toward the distance and struggles to quell an apprehension that something untoward might have befallen him.

Shameless points, flicking a kindly reassuring glance toward Polly as if acknowledging the depth of her concern. "It's all right, here he comes." She sighs in relief as they watch the approaching horse. Shameless adds with a note of surprise: "An' lookin' quite steady in the saddle."

"That's a worry," opines Polly with an eyebrow raised. "If <u>he's</u> steady in the saddle, it means he's overdone the fortifyin'."

"It's a good job he missed the hunt," opines the stablehand. "Might have added a few more homicides by accident. Well then," he says, clapping his hands together and allowing his pupils a last quick dart about, "everything ready?"

"Ready as it may be," says Polly. "Let's get to work."

They busy themselves in a last-minute flurry of food and drink service amongst the tables as the riders dismount. The salty air grows thick with chatter – mostly relating to the entirely fruitless hunt and the supposed closeness of the various participants to snaring the elusive fox. "He was in there, to be sure, but"… "I almost had him, but"… "If it weren't for"… All in all it's rather like a meeting of fishermen. Or tax inspectors.

Slowly, everyone moves inside the marquee to take up their assigned places for the "sombre formalities".

21. THE BOOK OF REVELATIONS

At the official table under the marquee, we sat sweltering in the heat as the Governor's brisk, businesslike speech concluded. I had taken in little or nothing of it, struggling to clear my mind from its tumultuous haze in readiness for my own perilous part in the proceedings to come.

"And so," uncle was saying, "before we hear more… er, heroic tales of exploration from Captain Ffeffington-Weekes," (several eyes roll at this exhilarating prospect) "I must first deal briefly with… rather more pressing business."

He drew a deep and meaningful breath and continued with steady deliberation: "As you are aware, this colony's third-ranking officer and my personal adjutant, Major Geoffrey Bascombe, was only days ago cut down by a cowardly assassin. By way of confirming that this colony is governed, and will continue to be governed, by the firm rule of law, the justice of the British Empire must now be done – and…"

Ffeffington-Weekes gave a loud tut-tut, shaking his head derisively: "Damned natives! I told you they can't be trusted."

The Reverend piped up, his voice suspiciously slurred: "I do hope the savage will be soundly *flogged* before we hang him?"

The Great Explorer chirped back: "Well, not much point in flogging him *afterwards,* eh Reverend?! Ha ha!" he chuckled loudly, delighted at his rapier wit.

"Oh Max, you *are* a wag!" fluttered Felicity, clutching his arm, the Captain beaming down at her with swaggering glee.

In the background I caught sight of Polly, utterly disgusted, rolling her eyes and mouthing in hysterical parody, "Max!?"

Blythe was glaring silently at all three speakers, annoyed at being so crassly and noisily interrupted at such an inappropriate juncture.

Reverend Staines returned his icy stare with a look of sheepish apology. "Merely asking, Excellency," he mumbled.

"Yes, well let us not get ahead of ourselves," warned the Governor. "As I said, justice must be done, so we must first hear the official finding of the inquest conducted by our Colonial Surgeon, Dr Quayle." He turned to me. "Doctor?"

I gulped, blinked, and rose rather unsteadily to my feet. I could almost feel Polly and Shameless waiting tensely in the background, stock still, eyes focused intently upon me.

There was no turning back now. The moment was upon us, the thing would have to be done. I could almost hear, once again, Davey's ghastly voice from the depths. *Down you come, sir!*

I shook my head. Yes, best get it over with.

"Er, thank you… Excellency," I began nervously, my voice cracking. "By the er, power of coronial inquiry vested in me by His Majesty's Government, I hereby announce… my er, findings on the death of… Major Geoffrey Bascombe, soldier in His Majesty's colonial forces."

All eyes were upon me. At the official table, my uncle, impatient and stern; next to him McMurdough, eyes downcast, alongside Anastasia, looking drawn and tense; The Reverend, red-rimmed eyes darting shiftily about; Felicity, smugly attached to the arm of her wild-eyed explorer; Dr Mountfort, puffing upon his pipe, ruddy face fixed implacably; Captain Partridge and other senior officers, all grim-faced; and an array of free settlers, all waiting in various states of dutiful attentiveness.

Behind them, Polly and Shameless stood watching me, he nodding encouragingly and she mouthing "Go on."

My head was swimming, whether or not from the tension of the moment or the delayed effect of the medicinal fortification, I cannot be sure.

Yes, now is the moment. Let us without further… *Come on now, sir! Before the next change of tide, if ye please!*

I swallowed and took a deep breath.

"Having investigated the circumstances of Major Bascombe's death, and… having taken evidence from witnesses duly sworn…"

"Get on with it!" hissed the Governor in a stage whisper.

Yes, now is the… "My finding is that… Major Bascombe met his demise at the hands of…er, of…"

My eyes flickered again over the overdressed personages. So many big fish in such a small pond, so many petty empires to be so desperately defended, so many schemes, so much duplicity seeking cover, so many a grubby motive scrabbling for its crime. I could understand now why it had been said that "The sun never sets upon the British Empire – because God doesn't trust them in the dark."

I gulped again. "…. er, was in fact m-murdered by…" My mouth had dried like the parched desert beyond the hills.

Down you come, sir! beckoned Davey inside my spinning head.

Shameless and Polly were practically nodding their heads off, willing me to finish the awful pronouncement.

"For God's sake, man, out with it!" barked my uncle.

I turned slowly to him and looked him directly in the eye. And I heard as if in some strange dream my own voice continuing, now oddly clear and steady:

"… by Sir Henry Blythe, Governor of Fort Portitude."

There were gasps from all around – and from nearby one of those damned birds cackled loudly, seeming to mock me. My only thought at this instant was to correct the unintended Spoonerism that had so dreadfully undermined my most dramatic moment, a correction which I attempted at once and in vain: "Er, Governor of Portit Fort… er," and I finally resolved with a huge gulp and almost inaudibly, "…er, Governor of this… colony."

And setting my chin in what I hoped would appear to be an attitude of quiet and rational resolution, I stared directly into the eyes of my uncle.

Immediately following my utterance of his name there had been an instant of deathly silence in which he did not react at all, his face fixed in its usual bluff, impatient expression. Then I fancied there was the tiniest flicker of the eyes, a flash of sudden and intense mental activity, as if all cogs therein were suddenly working in consort. A mere blink later, and this was replaced by a convincing expression of acute embarrassment. He coloured ever so slightly, but then regained his composure, fixed a steely grimace in place and hissed to me through the most menacingly clenched of teeth:

"Come come, Quayle, this is no time for juvenile japes." And he turned aside to those nearest him and muttered to them: "Had too much to drink. Smell it on his breath."

"Has he indeed? Shame!" hissed the Reverend at this, the impact of such condemnation rather diminished by the exuding of a loud belch. He hastily covered his mouth, sinking lower into his chair.

I raised my voice slightly, struggling to remain calm. "I am neither drunk nor in jest," I said. And facing my uncle squarely, I continued:

"You, Sir Henry, murdered Major Bascombe to stop him revealing your part in an enormous scheme of corrupt land grants... and the, er..."

My mind had gone blank for a moment, the enormity of the situation closing in upon me. Desperately I looked beyond the dignitaries towards Shameless – who was nodding frantically at me, miming skimming froth off a cup. One or two people, following my gaze, twisted about in their chairs – but Shameless deftly changed his movements to polishing a spot from the cup and averted his eyes from my direction.

"... and... what? Spilling?" I mumbled under my breath, as if engaged in a bizarre game of charades. "No, skimming, ah yes, of course..." and aloud, "...the ah, skimming of convict rations for personal profit – among various such schemes which have been continuing now, er, continuously, for more than..."

The Governor's face had now coloured to a deep crimson. He burst out angrily: "I think we've heard quite enough of this nonsense." He turned to McMurdough. "Colonel, have the Doctor removed to somewhere he may recover his wits."

McMurdough merely remained seated, eyes downcast. Blythe returned his gaze to me and almost spat with fury: "What in Heaven do you mean by this? By the Devil, I'll have you hanged, along with the blasted native!"

I looked again beyond the tables and saw Polly in an exaggerated mime of unfolding papers. I understood the gesture. Blythe, catching my gaze, spun around angrily to see what I was looking at. Others did likewise. At the instant of my comprehension, Polly changed her movement to one of swatting flies away from the food.

"I have evidence!" I shouted. "I have all the evidence necessary to prove every word!"

I reached inside my coat and withdrew the wad of selected documents. I dumped them emphatically upon the table in front of the Governor; and I continued more quietly, my eyes fixed upon him in horror as if upon some terrible, wounded beast:

"You'll find it's all there, uncle – all the falsified deeds, the hidden death certificates, all neatly signed in your own hand – every last fraudulent one. And all of it corroborated in considerable detail by…" and I flung it down on top of the documents: "the personal signed journal of Major Geoffrey Bascombe."

There were startled gasps, followed by a terrifyingly lengthy silence - broken finally by a loud hiccup from the Reverend.

Blythe stared down at the diary and the documents before him. His desperate expression conveyed to all that he was only too aware of what they contained. Behind the darting eyes his agile mind was racing desperately.

And then his voice came in a rushed gasp. "I knew nothing of this. *Nothing.*" He looked about, grasping at straws now. "It was Bascombe! *He* did it – he did all of it! I… I tried to stop him, of course…"

"No," I shook my head, "it was all your idea. You, sir, were the mastermind - Bascombe was merely your agent. His bitter envy made him your easy target. You promised to reward him at last for all the slights and injustices he felt he had endured throughout his career. Everything was kept in his name, but you made certain the cream of the spoils came to you.

"Whether he kept this diary merely as an outlet for his feelings of guilt, or as some kind of insurance against you, I know not, but for whatever reason, he recorded every detail. It's all in here." I held the diary aloft as I continued:

"And when the colonial surgeon, Dr Helfcott, stumbled upon one of your bogus land grants and sought an explanation from you, your response was to set Bascombe onto him. The Major knew the Doctor's early morning clifftop riding routine and was in a perfect position to sneak into the stable late at night and cut the saddle strap almost through – with the intended consequence.

"And when we…" I glanced at Polly and Shameless, who were shaking their heads fiercely. I corrected myself hurriedly: "… er, that is, I should say, when *I* unearthed the evidence of that murder, and made the mistake of alerting the Major to it by my inquiries into the process of granting land…" and at this point I found myself staring directly at Anastasia McMurdough who immediately averted her gaze, "Bascombe came rushing to you in a panic."

I now seized and opened the diary at a carefully bookmarked page. "Let me quote from his journal, written on the very day of his death:

Today is the day. I shall inform the Governor this very evening that our little arrangement is over. I will do no more of his killing, no more of his larceny, I will have no more of any of it. I will be out of the whole damned mess.

I met now, as squarely as I could manage, my uncle's blazing eyes. "But you, Sir Henry, you knew there was to be only one way out for Major Bascombe. You could not allow him to reveal your commanding role in this whole scheme of unthinkable villainy."

There now came to me a vivid flashback of the words my uncle had spoken so forcefully to me upon our first meeting in his office: *I am determined to make Port Fortitude a great and lasting settlement – and Heaven help the man who stands in the way of that aim. Do I make myself clear?* He had certainly made himself clear in the manner in which he had removed first the troublesome Helfcott and then the quibbling Bascombe from his path.

Fired up now perhaps, I must admit, by a grim sense of revenge for all the humiliating rebukes, lectures and insults I had suffered from this hypocrite, I drove onwards towards my conclusion:

"On the appointed evening, you removed the native spear from Ffeffington-Weekes' collection in the ballroom, and proceeded to your secret rendezvous with the Major - from my examination of whose body, I concluded that the spear was thrust upwards through his ribcage…" I paused for effect here and uttered the remaining words with contempt I can hardly have disguised: "… by a person of *diminutive stature.*"

This last insult was too much for Blythe. His face contorted into a snarl as he bellowed: "How *dare* you!" And looking wildly about, his eyes fixed again on his military subordinate, still sitting motionless next to him, eyes downcast.

"McMurdough," he thundered, "what the devil are you sitting there for? I ordered you to *arrest* this mutinous lunatic! Arrest him at *once!*"

I turned to McMurdough with calm expectation. "Well, Colonel?" I prompted quietly.

Slowly, Montague McMurdough rose from his seat and put on his military hat, the dark curl protruding from beneath it making him appear, I thought, rather like that young French general, whose name I could not bring to mind at this rather tense juncture. Slowly he raised his eyes and fixed them steadily upon his superior.

"I think not," he said simply.

"What!?" Blythe almost choked, face a vivid purple. "Do you... are you *disobeying* me?"

McMurdough, looking directly into the Governor's eyes as if seeing him for the first time, continued quietly and without the faintest hint of fear: "Having already examined this journal, and the other evidence, I find it makes a compelling case against you. I am afraid it leaves me no alternative."

And watched in open-mouthed amazement by all, not least his wife – who seemed quite unwilling to believe that her husband could possibly be capable of any decisive act, let alone one of such staggering import – Colonel McMurdough stepped forward, and as we had planned at our meeting the previous day, unrolled a document from which he read calmly:

"Sir Henry Blythe, I declare you unfit to govern under Section 247(b) of the Colonial Administration Act of 1766. Under its provisions I hereby assume command of this Colony, and arrest you in the name of the King."

Over the shocked murmurs of the assemblage, he looked again very steadily at Blythe. "You will be returned to England to face trial. Come along quietly now, sir." And at this he gave the Governor the very faintest of half-smiles, cemented in the most implacable resolution.

There were several heartbeats of pure crystalline tension. Then all seemed to shatter at once.

First Felicity shrieked, aghast: "Papa, how *could* you!" Ffeffington-Weekes immediately cast a protective arm around her and glared in appropriate outrage at the disgraced Governor.

The latter cast his eyes about wildly, looking for any avenue of deliverance. He found none, armed troopers now having converged smoothly around him at McMurdough's pre-arranged direction, Captain Partridge at their head looking characteristically unflappable though for once without his trademark grin.

It all seemed to happen in an instant. Suddenly Blythe drew the pistol like lightning from his waistband. Reaching across the table, he grabbed Anastasia and twisted his body behind hers, holding the firearm to her temple and backing away from the throng. The troopers raised their weapons towards him.

I threw my hands up. "Wait!" I screamed. "Colonel, tell your men to hold their fire!"

Anastasia's face was a taut, skeletal snarl of terror, the Governor's gun at her head. This was something of an achievement, since she was considerably taller than he; his only means of overcoming this was to grab the back of her hair and pull downwards, bending the poor woman over backwards at a most ungainly angle.

I looked at McMurdough. A strange expression flickered across his face for a moment at this vision - one almost of satisfaction at his domineering wife's predicament. He paused for a significant moment, eyes more alight than I had ever seen them.

Then, not without a tinge of reluctance, he finally agreed: "Oh, all right. Hold your fire!" And I fancy I heard him add under his breath: "Damn it."

"Yes," warned Blythe, "very wise. And keep your distance – for this…" (with a sneer) " 'good lady's' sake. Hah!"

Now he smirked, maintaining his grip on the squirming Anastasia as he raised his voice to scoff at us.

"So you think you've 'found me out', do you? Well, I've found *you* out – all of you." He flashed his eyes around at his tormentors. "Small-minded people – all your petty schemes paled into insignificance alongside *my* grand vision for this colony. A colony none of you would have been fit to live in!"

We could do nothing but remain frozen as he glowered at us, then turned with ferocity towards me.

"And you – hell-bent on being such a hero, eh? Just like your blasted father - damn him! Well, for all my dear brother-in-law's naval heroics, I would have grown so much larger than he could ever have been – if you hadn't come stumbling in here, wrecking everything. Years of meticulous planning – all of it dashed!

"Well," he smirked, looking around at the multitude, "you may have destroyed this colony's chance for greatness – but you're not big enough to take *me* – none of you!"

He had backed toward the horses. He suddenly flung Anastasia roughly to the ground, raised his pistol and fired in our direction.

Everyone ducked, leapt or simply fainted where they stood. Miraculously, the shot missed human flesh completely, smashing a wine flask. Its contents splashed liberally upon the smock of the Chaplain, who wiped his hand across it, licking his fingers with approval.

Then, before anyone had recovered sufficiently to respond, the deranged Governor had leapt onto the nearest horse and thundered off at full gallop towards the bush.

22. FULL CIRCLE

Ignoring the prostrate Anastasia's feeble cry of "Montague!", McMurdough shouted "After him!" to the troopers.

They hesitated as Ffeffington-Weekes bellowed: "Oh, let him be – where can he go? Out *there*, in the wilderness? You'd have to be *mad!*" And with this he grinned insanely - but the grin faded quickly as he became embarrassingly aware, from the smirks and nods of agreement that greeted this, that his unwitting self-condemnation had met with near-universal endorsement.

McMurdough now spoke again, sharply, with something of his new-found decisiveness: "There's a trading vessel in port, East India man, leaving for California within the hour. He'll be headed for the docks. After him - at once!"

Now Partridge and the other soldiers dashed for the horses, McMurdough and Ffeffington-Weekes with them.

Before they reached their mounts I became aware of hooves right next to me. Polly, already mounted, had ridden up beside me, her eyes aflame with courage.

From behind me, I heard Felicity's cry of "Max!" and the prostrate Anastasia's irritated repetition of *"Montague!"* And I glimpsed over my shoulder the Reverend Staines hovering lecherously over her, fighting off Dr Mountfort's attempted assistance, loudly protesting that he, the Reverend, was the best one to minister to the lady's needs - the first imperative being, he insisted, to loosen her clothing a little.

"Here, Doctor! Come on!" shouted Polly - and before I knew it, she had reached down and grasped my hand, pulling me almost effortlessly up behind her. I gave a startled cry as we hurtled towards the bush.

Not daring to look ahead, I lowered my head and glanced under my arm at the scene behind us. I caught a tantalising glimpse of Ffeffington-Weekes dashing heroically towards his horse and leaping into the saddle – or at least this is what he intended, but in his eagerness to impress Felicity he overshot his target and went hurtling straight over the top with a wild squawk. Something from Shakespeare came immediately to mind about "vaulting ambition o'erleaping itself and falling on th' other side" – but I had barely an instant to enjoy this comical event before there was a lurch from our mount, and Polly and I were in under the twisted canopy of the trees, ducking low as random branches whipped past on all sides, slashing at our faces.

Glancing back again, I could see that we were several lengths ahead of McMurdough, Partridge, and the remaining troopers. I could do naught but hang on for dear life – more so as the track emerged from the dense foliage and opened out onto a narrow clifftop ledge, which we hurtled onto with such speed that I feared we must surely plunge from its lip and onto the jagged rocks and frothing breakers far below. *Down you come, sir!* hooted the imaginary Mr Jones.

I closed my eyes and clung to Polly as if my life depended upon it – which in fact I am sure it did; but somewhere behind the terror and the nausea came the barely conscious recognition that I was almost – though possibly not quite – as concerned for her safety as for my own. I had, however, barely an instant to ponder the significance of this lurking sentiment before she, demonstrating extraordinary expertise, reined our mount sharply to a halt, her determined eyes darting to left and right in search of our quarry.

"There he is! 'ang on!" she shouted – as if I needed any encouragement to do that - and we were off at a brisk clip along the clifftop track once more, my vitals boiling up in protest.

We were soon at full gallop, the hooves raising sparks from the rocky outcrop beneath us. Up ahead, Blythe turned to look over his shoulder, and seeing us in close pursuit, whipped his steed onward. I could hear, well behind us, the hooves of the pursuing troopers, above the incessant crashing of the waves against the cliffs. All of these sounds barely overshadowed the inward rumble marking the growing discord within my own stomach.

We came thundering around a bend in the track, dust and sparks flying - and in an instant we skidded suddenly and noisily to a dead halt, I grasping desperately for purchase upon poor Polly's hair and garments to avoid tumbling off. Once I had miraculously recovered my balance, I lifted my head to stare in amazement at the extraordinary tableau ahead.

Several yards in front of us, the Governor had pulled up stock still - finding his way completely blocked by – yes, no mistaking that shape – it was none other than Carmel. And lounging nonchalantly upon the dromedary's back, as cool as a cucumber, was the comfortable figure of Seamus Halloran.

His drawling brogue hung lazily in the salty air. "And where might you be goin' now, Your Less-Than-Excellency?"

"Stand aside!" bellowed the Governor after a moment of double-take, and he levelled his pistol at the convict's head, squinting murderously along its barrel as he took aim.

My heart leapt to my mouth. "Noooo!" I bellowed.

Shameless, however, was not the least bit alarmed. "You've already fired that," he observed calmly; but was nevertheless unable to suppress the momentary reflex of ducking as the Governor pulled on the trigger, its dull click confirming the relieved stablehand's ballistic analysis. He beamed smugly.

Purple with fury, Blythe hurled the pistol at Halloran, who ducked again, the weapon missing both him and the camel and crashing into the bush beyond.

This last provocation, however, was altogether too much for Carmel, whose patience could only be extended so far. She lifted her head, gave an angry snort and advanced one defiant step towards the Governor. This caused the latter's horse to rear and bolt sideways – straight down the steep embankment towards the cliff.

We watched in horror, as if in some too brightly lit nightmare, as the villain hurtled down the embankment as if upon some legendary mountain ride, reins clutched maniacally in one hand, the other flailing wildly behind him – until at the very edge of the cliff the horse stopped dead… and bucked.

Sir Henry Blythe went straight over his mount's head and tumbled like a circus clown into oblivion, his scream fading into the endless snarling of the waves beneath.

Polly urged us cautiously forwards now, and we came up next to Shameless and Carmel, the hooves of McMurdough and the rest now rumbling up behind us.

Something else was also rumbling up. I looked down at the awful finality of what lay below, and felt Polly's arm reaching reassuringly around my shoulders; but I could not help myself – I pushed her arm away, turned my head aside and was violently ill as I had never been ill before, not even at sea.

Just below us on the clifftop, the riderless horse stood in silhouette, whinnying gently towards the unforgiving ocean.

23. THE HANG OF THE PLACE

Majestic masts stood once more in the sparkling bay of Port Fortitude in the full bright flower of a fresh Antipodean morning, the sun streaming across the sparkling waters.

The tall ship stood peacefully at anchor, its cream sails furled. The unloading of its passengers and cargo was now all but finished – new settlers and new convicts bustling ashore to begin new lives, boxes and crates hauled off up the track, creatures scampered off into the bush. Now the ship stood waiting as if a mother duck for its wayward ducklings: a flotilla of longboats at the jetty and upon the beach beginning to load passengers and cargo for the much shorter voyage around the coast to the larger settlement of Sydney Cove, and from there in due course back to England.

Gathered upon the jetty were an assortment of people who, for a diversity of reasons, were leaving Port Fortitude – mostly forever. Some had completed a term of duty or sentence and were either returning to the more established settlement, or were heading back to what they must still have thought of as "home" – perhaps for a long-anticipated reunion with family, friends or careers.

Others were making a more definite choice to return to the old world, whether having found their absence from it too painful, or perhaps having been defeated by the harsh circumstances of life in the colonies.

My eyes were fixed upon the ship as I walked slowly down to the pier, deep in thought. Reaching the jetty, I detected among the convicts, settlers, soldiers and sailors bustling about, the familiar battered straw hat and generously-proportioned figure of Shameless Halloran.

He was whistling another of his dreadful ditties, but - perhaps in consideration of our differing musical tastes - stopped immediately as he looked up to see me. Possibly noticing that I was a little more neatly dressed than usual, he appeared rather surprised.

"You here, Your Doctorship?" He raised one eyebrow and inquired, I fancied just a little apprehensively, "Not thinkin' of goin' back, are yer?"

I must admit there was a moment's hesitation. The thought of England, with its cool and bracing weather, its green rolling hills, its familiar townships and farmlands – these recollections were by no means unwelcome.

This, however, passed in a mere instant. One can never go back, not really. One must move on, and make the best of things. "No, no," I hastened to reassure him, "I'm just… keeping an eye out for… Felicity."

Now he raised the other eyebrow to join its unruly partner, and snorted derisively. "Not still keen on *her*, are yer?"

I shook my head sagely. "Oh no, indeed not, I've well and truly gotten over that foolishness. But she is after all, my cousin, and… well, I am concerned at how she is coping with the tragedy and trauma of losing her father…."

At this point, as if on cue, and saving me from further nausea-inducing thoughts of those recent cataclysmic events, the young lady in question came bustling importantly towards the jetty, upon the arm of her Great Explorer. I noted with repressed glee his other arm suspended in a sling – the result of his ludicrous equestrian mishap. Both he and his companion were impeccably overdressed, she prattling incessantly as always.

"I shall tell you one thing – I will not be sorry to get away from this dashed heat! Honestly, I can quite understand why Papa went mad, Max dear… I mean the climate alone would drive anyone quite insane…"

"Yes, well it's the confounded convict element I can't stand," lisped her pommaded paramour bitterly. "Would you believe it - even my camel, my loyal ship of the desert, has been purloined, it seems, under my very nose."

"Poor darling", she cooed, clasping her arm around him - rather too firmly for the comfort of his injured limb, thereby eliciting a squawk of pain. She made no apology but merely withdrew her arm impatiently and grasped his uninjured one more firmly as they drew alongside me.

I stepped forward and ventured quietly: "Dear cousin Felicity... I do hope you are... bearing up... under the terrible..."

She brushed me aside with a dismissive wave of the arm and that characteristic pout. "Yes yes, quite well enough thank you... now come *on*, Max dear, we must get aboard, it's almost time for aperitifs...." And with that, they were off along the jetty and scuttling into the longboat.

Shameless came sauntering up beside me. "She seems to be, er, 'bearin' up' all right, Doctor. Not too 'traumatised', by the look o' things."

"No, indeed not," I agreed with a wry smirk.

"Well, if you'll excuse my presumptuousness, bein' shot of her from your life is what I'd call... a happy feat", my friend concluded; and I could not but agree.

We watched in silence as the sailors heaved upon the oars and the longboat pulled away towards the ship.

"Not wishin' you were aboard, then?" prodded my comrade, squinting at me. "Headin' back to good old Mother England?"

"What," I exclaimed in horror, "and endure another sea voyage? *Never.*"

My only contribution to this vessel's cargo had been a rather long letter sent home to my mother. In it, I outlined, as fully but as gently as I was able to, the recent dramatic course of events; and I commiserated with her in the loss of her brother.

I had softened the account somewhat by attributing his deranged behaviour to some sort of mental breakdown, which I couched in authoritatively medical terminology. I did not, of course, mention his tirade against my late father. I sought to assure Mother in the most fervent terms that whatever disgrace the family might suffer by association from Sir Henry's fall, I would seek to overcome in the fullness of time by my own earnest endeavours to consolidate a respectable, and indeed a noteworthy career in the Antipodes. I trusted that she would be at least relieved that her son had at last shown due courage in the line of duty; and I concluded the letter by averring that I was determined to maintain this high standard of behaviour – the kind of conduct that would make her, and would have made my dear father, proud.

I did not add what I really felt, which was that I was not at all confident that I would be able to live up to any of these lofty pronouncements; nor did I confide that it was only by the most felicitous of fortune that I had managed even to survive thus far.

Well, that is to say, fortune and… yes, friendship. I looked over at Shameless with a slight pang of guilt. Another significant omission from my letter had been any mention whatsoever of the fact that the defeat of my demented uncle had been achieved in close consort with two convicts. This was not, I felt, an omission that could have been avoided. Their courageous part in the final chase was witnessed and recognised; but their guiding role in the whole investigation must remain forever a secret, not only from my mother but from all members of the "respectable" classes, fully understood and appreciated only by the three of us - and of course, Jacky.

"No," I concluded definitely to Shameless, "there'll be no return voyage for me. I shall see out my commission here; and perhaps even earn myself a nice… land grant."

He looked at me sharply and I immediately held up my hand, adding hurriedly: "A strictly *legal* one – from whoever may be governing us at that juncture; and remaining, I trust, well within the law."

At this moment the new Acting Governor of Port Fortitude, Colonel Montague McMurdough, sits back in his chair behind the big oak desk once occupied by his predecessor.

Gone from the wall behind him is the so-much-larger-than-life portrait of the late and unlamented Sir Henry Blythe. Hastily mounted in its place, a very large framed painting of a prize ram. This must suffice until the artistic services of Mr Patterson can once more be engaged - and his keen eye for realism once more grudgingly subdued. Under Anastasia's inflexible and relentless direction, her husband's passing resemblance to the handsome young General Bonaparte will be well emphasised in the ensuing portrait, though it will not be mentioned in the presence of its Francophobic subject.

The Great Lady herself stands now immediately behind Montague. Decidedly Lady Macbeth-like, her hard and handsome face smirking in grim satisfaction.

We have been fortunate, she thinks, most fortunate. The young doctor wisely chose to overlook those… how had he described them so diplomatically?…

"inadvertent administrative irregularities" in some of our own business transactions - in the interests, presumably, of garnering the necessary support for the snaring of his bigger fish. A most prudent decision, she thinks. He has more wit than I had expected – or else he was well advised in the matter.

She has a strong suspicion that the latter was the case – and she believes she knows where such advice might have originated from. However, she determines, that is best left alone for now - especially since, she shudders, the young doctor for his strategic reasons also withheld from Montague certain… details, particularly relating to my little indiscretion with the late Major. Perhaps in this case, the secrets of the doctor and ourselves might best be left to lie undisturbed, for our mutual benefit. And that of the colony, of course, she adds hastily to herself. Since we must now, ebven more than before, have the colony's best interests at heart. Or at least appear to.

One must move forwards, she determines with a clenching of her noble jaw. There are important matters to attend to.

Following her narrow escape, at least for the moment, from what might have proved a most unfortunate line of enquiry, Milady is now already planning the first of several months' worth of delicate political manoeuvres. These include the eliciting and despatch of letters of support, testimonials, the inducement of quiet words in the right ears – all of which must be expertly executed if she's to transform her husband's temporary promotion into a permanent one. First Lady of the colony – now this, she thinks, is a position I could well live with.

Anastasia looks down at Montague and one corner of her thin mouth curls up just slightly. *Who would have thought,* she wonders silently, *that he had that kind of fortitude in him? For such a display of character she might almost forgive him for that most culpable moment of hesitation in disarming his men while the lunatic was threatening her. That transgression she will not let her husband hear the last of, not in a hurry. It will be filed in her categorical mind and produced when it will best serve.*

The Acting Governor is oblivious all this. His mind is more than fully occupied with examining an artistic representation of a distinctly ugly creature he plans to introduce to the settlement in an attempt to control a certain beetle which has been found to be a threat to sugarcane. This is a crop that, at his wife's suggestion, he intends to establish here in the very near future - in order to produce some real rum, saleable at a far more lucrative price than the cheap gin that has so far passed for it. The crop must be protected. And this creature, he determines, will do it.

Under the picture is the legend "THE CANE TOAD." Its loathsome, knobbly visage grins up from the page, as if anticipating the splendid mischief it's destined to wreak upon the hapless continent.

There's a loud CRACK! from outside the window. And a scream. And the dimly audible sound of a chubby clerical fist smacked gleefully into the palm of an equally chubby hand.

Life goes on in His Majesty's Colony of Port Fortitude.

"Don't suppose you could use some 'elp, could yer?"

The voice woke me from my daydream of land grant and quiet pastoral future. A familiar and welcome female voice, its Cockney lilt sliding softly over the din of dockside bustle. I turned towards the robust figure and its dimpled smile, tilting my head in faint enquiry.

"On the farm, like," she explained - and added with that most appealing thrust of the chin and that most engaging spark of fire in the eye, "I'm good with 'orses."

"I've noticed," I agreed with intended neutrality, but somehow unable to keep the growing admiration from my voice. I smiled back at her, and I fancied our smiles connected and became, for a moment, indefinably greater than the sum of their two parts.

"I do think you were very brave," she opined. "It don't come natural-like to you, but it may be that makes it even braver."

I could do nothing but blush and continue smiling at her. It occurred to me that she had now seen me half-drowned, drunk, and violently ill – and if after all that, she could still smile at me in that rather disarming fashion, well then, perhaps there was hope for me yet.

"Hah! Go on, you two!" came Shameless's delighted cackle. "Ahhh, if I was five years younger…" And he gave her a mock leer.

"Get away with yer," she chided.

"All right then… seven," he determined in mock bargain. "An' that's me final offer."

"Only females you'd be interested in for any length o' time, Shameless 'Alloran, would need to 'ave four legs, a tail, an' a good sale price."

Unwilling or unable to dispute this, he grinned and turned away to peer purposefully towards the ship. "Great Explorer gone aboard, then?"

I squinted towards the vessel. "Gone below, I fancy. No sign of him on deck."

"Right then." He stepped back along the jetty and whistled loudly.

There was a formidable rustle in the bushes - and from thence emerged Carmel, loaded up with tools and provisions, in front of which sat Jacky, smiling serenely.

"Shameless!", I turned to him severely. "You didn't..." I gestured to the camel and back towards the ship.

He nodded slowly and earnestly. "Call it compensation - for the wrongful imprisonment." And at this he brought his finger up to his lips.

Polly and I followed Shameless up the beach to meet Carmel, who lumbered placidly to a halt under her new master's assured handling. Polly called up to him: "Not stayin' with us, then, Jacky?"

"No more to learn here," he sighed, shaking his dark curls. "No offence, but... cannot see your colony amount to much." And he added with gentle apology: "You people not have... *hang* of the place, eh."

Shameless chuckled. "Possibly not, friend," he was forced to concede; and I wondered whether indeed we would ever have the "hang of the place".

"Farewell then," said Jacky – and then with a broad grin: "Thanks for... 'horse'."

We laughed and waved - a small tear, I noticed, coming to the eye of Shameless at the departure of not one but two friends.

Carmel gave a snort, and Jacky half-turned as they moved away to call out over his shoulder: "Best of British luck!"

"Thank you!" we called back to him.

And Polly murmured with conviction (convictions, I could not help thinking with an inward smirk, being something she well understood): "We shall bloody well need it."

We watched as camel and rider loped off in the direction of the scrub.

Behind us the great sails rose and fluttered into fullness as they were picked up by the fresh breeze, and the ship began to slide slowly away toward the mouth of the harbour, ready to negotiate the hazardous reefs beyond.

We three stood silently upon the sand at the edge of the great unknown continent, ourselves a small ship of trust and companionship surrounded by a treacherous ocean of deviousness - well, at least, all things considered, in the circumstances, of far greater deviousness than anything we could ever aspire to.

After a moment I turned toward Shameless, perhaps to convey something of this sentiment; but his attention had already been diverted, his mind once more upon the main chance. He was speaking to someone behind him, a new arrival left upon the jetty, struggling to shift an item of heavy luggage.

"Don't worry about that trunk, sir – it'll be safe here," assured that familiar brogue. He turned to wink at us, pupils darting: "Safe as houses…"

I opened my mouth to express some disapproval at this all too familiar phrase and its implications, but Polly stopped me by putting her finger to my lips.

Very well, I nodded in silent agreement. To each his small frailty – and some are best left where they lie.

As the seabirds swooped and soared, their laments filling the salty air, I allowed Polly to grasp my arm firmly and lead me off up the beach toward the strange, twisting trees - leaving Shameless Halloran, convict investigator, unraveller of mysteries, to go about his… other business.

THE END

THE WRITER

Stafford Sanders is or has been a writer, journalist, media advocate, satirist, teacher and musician.

He graduated from Macquarie University with Honours in English Literature and studies in British and Australian History.

He has written satirical comedy for ABC-TV's *BackBerner* and prolifically for ABC, SBS and community radio networks – including colonial history satires (with co-storywriter Tony Latimore). Some of his sketches were released on the 2000 ABC Audio CD *The Millennium Bagged by John Behinde and Friends*.

Stafford's radio writings and reports have appeared across the US and Australia and have won many awards - including a Pater World Broadcasting Award, an International Radio Festival silver medal, a national BASF Radio Comedy Award and a Sir William McKell Award for Environmental Broadcasting.

He has also written successful comedies for the stage - for Sydney's New Theatre and Canberra's Upfront (winning Best Script at the ACT Playwrights' Festival); and for schools - his musical *The Lizard of Oz* performed by primary schools across Australia.

His songs have been recorded, published and won prizes. Songs written with the group "Men With Day Jobs" have been covered in the US, Canada and Australia, used as university teaching resources, and notched up many thousands of YouTube hits.

Along the way he has taught at schools and universities, reported from the Amazon, tackled Big Tobacco, campaigned for the rights of renters and people seeking asylum, raised three children, and once performed on pop show *Countdown* in a sailor suit.

ACKNOWLEDGMENTS

I wish to acknowledge the very valuable collaboration of Tony Latimore on the original story and feature screenplay of *Bloody Colonials* – including his conception of the character of Shameless Halloran.

I'm also very grateful for their critical input to friends and authors Frankie Seymour (*All Hearts on Deck*), Dr Julie Browning (*Dynasties*) and Gary Bryson (*Turtle*); and to the following for their creative/critical contributions: Lucy Browning, Kea Browning, Rebecca Browning, Rod Crundwell, Janet de Bres, Suzy McKenzie, Celeste Pena, Charlie Sanders, Dr John Sanders, Kim Sanders, and Dominic Stone.

www.ingramcontent.com/pod-product-compliance
Lightning Source LLC
Chambersburg PA
CBHW071359290426
44108CB00014B/1616